PILGRIMS IN HINDU

Cover illustration: Nalikanta (21,713 ft) at the head of the Rishiganga Valley.

The milestone at Rudraprayag.

Pilgrims in Hindu Holy Land:
Sacred Shrines of the Indian Himalayas

Geoffrey Waring Maw

edited by
Gillian M. (Maw) Conacher
and Marjorie Sykes

Sessions Book Trust
York, England

ISBN 1 85072 190 4

Dedication

I would like to dedicate this book to Geoffrey Maw's eight grand-children, Leila Straus and Antony Maw, Ian and Neil Conacher, David and Richard Maw and their sister Christine Coventry, with a special tribute to Diana Maw, whose life was taken from her too soon, and whose friendship I miss still.

Along with my brother Hugh, and sister-in-law Nahia, I am deeply grateful to them all for their support and encouragement.

Last, but most, thankyou to my husband for his patience, advice and painstaking attention to detail, and putting up with the many happy hours I spent in my father's footsteps in the Himalayas.

GILLIAN M. (MAW) CONACHER
March 1997

Printed in 11 on 12 point Plantin Typeface
by Sessions of York
The Ebor Press
York, England

Contents

Illustrations

Editor's Foreword

THE AUTHOR OF THIS BOOK reached India in 1910, and for the next 39 years, he and his wife worked as missionaries of the Society of Friends in what is now Madhya Pradesh. During the first years spent in Hoshangabad District, many factors combined to focus Geoffrey Maw's interest on the spiritual aspirations of those who travel the pilgrim ways. Hoshangabad town itself stands on the south bank of the great and sacred Narmada river. By the riverside temples and on the bathing *ghats sadhus* and pilgrims were always to be found. A few miles upstream the Tawa river joins the Narmada, and many thousands of devotees gather annually at the confluence for a great bathing festival. Among the hills to the south, where the Tawa rises, is the mountain shrine of Mahadeo, the 'great god' Shiva, where also the pilgrims throng. The Friends, Indian and British, attended such festivals to share with the pilgrims their own spiritual experiences of an inward Teacher, the living 'Christ' in the heart.

In 1916 Geoffrey and Mildred Maw went back to England for a year's leave. While they were away the young Christian *sannyasi*, Sadhu Sundar Singh, visited Hoshangabad and made a very deep impression on all its people. The news reached the Maws early in 1917. Later that year, in view of the risks of war-time travel, they agreed that Geoffrey should return to India alone, leaving Mildred and the children in England. He took with him to read on the voyage an account of Sundar Singh's way of life. He later read another book, the description of how Dr Pennell ('Pennell of the Afghan Frontier') had lived for a time as a *sadhu* in Rishikesh.

There followed three momentous years. The people of Hoshangabad District, their powers of resistance undermined by near-famine conditions, suffered very severely in the influenza epidemic of the closing months of 1918. In their desperate need,

Geoffrey Maw's most sensitive Indian friends longed for a renewed and deeper spiritual experience. The war ended, and early in 1919 two young English Friends reached India, seeking a way to share their religious experience not as paid 'missionaries', but as ordinary working men earning their living with their own hands. Their brief visit to Hoshangabad inspired one of Geoffrey's trusted Indian colleagues to do the same. This was Khushilal, whose family were traditional Hindu exorcists in a rural area near Hoshangabad. He had joined the Friends in his youth and had become a leader of the mission. He now renounced his mission pay, earned what he needed by manual labour, and donned the ochre robe of the *sadhu*. By 1920 Geoffrey, similarly clad, was accompanying him on short journeys on foot among the villages in the area. In 1921 they went for the first time to a great festival outside their own district, the Kumbh Mela at Ujjain, and mingled with some of the many thousands of *sadhus* assembled there.

From that time forward, Geoffrey and Khushilal dreamed of the Himalayan pilgrimages. Inquiries were made, plans were laid, and in 1923 they undertook the first of the pilgrimages described in this book. In that year Mildred Maw, who had rejoined her husband in India in 1919, returned to England with their children, and Geoffrey was free from family duties. The later pilgrimages were made in similar conditions.

Geoffrey Maw kept a journal of his experiences, and during the 1950s hoped and planned to publish a book. For a number of reasons this did not prove possible during his lifetime. The present volume retains his original wording, with a very few minor changes; the nomenclature then in general use, before the re-organisation of the Indian States which followed Independence, has been retained. The chief editorial modification is to assemble the 'general' material in an introductory Part I, leaving the particular incidents of the various pilgrimages to be described in the appropriate place.

GILLIAN M. (MAW) CONACHER
March 1997

For Indian words see Glossary, pages 162-165.

PART I
INTRODUCTION TO THE PILGRIMAGES

CHAPTER 1

The Author's Experience

'The sacrifices that are made in order to please the gods can only be performed by rajas, maharajas, and other wealthy people, because for the right performance of these sacrifices quantities of materials and vast wealth are needed, and it is beyond the capacity of common folk to make such sacrifices. For this reason the saints and seers ordained regulations for the right performance of pilgrimages, so that the same merit might accrue to ordinary people as to those who perform burnt sacrifices.'

(Mahabharata)

THIS BOOK RECORDS MY experiences on the great Hindu pilgrimage route to the sources of the Ganges.

Why did I go? I am a foreigner and a Christian, and much of my active life has been spent working for the Society of Friends (Quakers) in the Hoshangabad District of the Central Provinces. There I tried to understand the aspirations and achievements of Hindu religious life; I focused my interest on the pilgrims, and especially the *sadhus* who congregate at the holy places and along the sacred ways. I found that if I were to understand them I must know for myself something of the life of the pilgrim way. During some of my hot-weather holidays I have therefore gone on pilgrimages, and among my travels I have included this most famous pilgrimage of all.

I joined the pilgrimage on four occasions, in 1923, 1930, 1934 and 1948. In 1923 I travelled first to Kedarnath, then over the

Chobta Pass to Chamoli and on to Badrinath. I returned down the Alaknanda river as far as Karnprayag, where I made a detour to Pauri, and went back thence to Hardwar. In 1930 I did an extra march from Badrinath in the direction of the actual source of the Alaknanda, and on my return followed the Ganges route to Hardwar. In 1934 I repeated the 1930 journey, and in 1948 I did a shortened pilgrimage to Badrinath only, going by bus and lorry along the new motor road as far as Nandprayag; the walk was thus reduced from the full 450 to a mere 108 miles.

In essentials the pilgrimage does not change. The route remains the same, apart from minor detours caused by landslides; the road is opened and closed about the same time each year. Pilgrimages differ only in details of companions, weather, health and the like.

Yet in my time one major change was coming over the pilgrimage – its mechanisation. On my first three journeys I went on foot; the only alternative was to be carried by *coolies* in a *kandi* (basket) or a *dandi* (sedan-chair) which was repugnant to my moral sense and also beyond my pocket. But I walked not only because I had to, but also because I wished to share as nearly as possible the life of the great majority of pilgrims. In 1948 circumstances were changing, and I was very glad of the saving in labour and time. I had no time that year for a full pilgrimage, and I was anxious to have a longer stay at Badrinath with various old friends; above all, the arthritis which on earlier pilgrimages had given me increasing pain, had by then reached a stage which made the full journey physically impossible.

Eventually there will be a through motor-road to Badrinath. Sooner or later there will be landing-grounds at Badrinath and Kedarnath, providing a regular service by air. I do not suppose that mechanisation will kill the pilgrimage, but I am glad to have known it in the days when it was a full physical feat of walking. A mechanised pilgrimage can never remain the adventure of body and spirit that it was for my companions of the way when I first trod it with them.

The experiences recorded in this book are thus probably unique. American and Europeans have indeed traversed the route as mountaineers, explorers, sportsmen or missionaries, but none, I think, in the way that I have done, as a *sadhu* among *sadhus*, sharing in the pilgrimage in some measure from the pilgrim's point of view, as a religious event. Perhaps now no-one else ever will, so swift are the technological, political and spiritual changes sweeping over India. I have had a share in something that was unique in the world, that was in many ways a fine thing – a great spiritual quest pursued in lovely places; as such it is worthy of record.

CHAPTER 2

The Purpose of the Pilgrimage

Yudhishthira enquired from Bhishma: 'What is considered the foremost of all *tirthas*? What is that *tirtha* which conduces to the greatest Purity?' Bhishma replied, 'All *tirthas* are possessed of merit. Listen, however, as I tell you what the *tirtha*, the cleanser, is of men gifted with wisdom. Following eternal Truth one should bathe in the *tirtha* called Manasa, which is unfathomable, stainless and pure, and which has Truth for its waters and the understanding for its lake. The fruits, in the form of cleansing, that one gains by bathing in that *tirtha*, are freedom from cupidity, sincerity, truthfulness, mildness, mercy, abstention from injuring any creature, self-control and tranquillity.
(Mahabharata, Anushasana Parva. Chap. CVIII, 1-8.)

INDIA IS A LAND OF pilgrimages, every orthodox Hindu is a potential pilgrim. Sooner or later, to rich and poor, to priest and peasant, comes the urge to lay aside the cares and troubles of everyday life and ancestral calling, pack his brass platter and drinking vessel and one or two other indispensable oddments in a cloth bag, tie the few silver *rupees* that are his life savings in a knot in a corner of his loin cloth and secrete it in the folds round his waist, shoulder the little bundle of change of clothing and a blanket, grasp a stout stick and set out into the unknown to seek the vision of God.

There are sacred places all over India; the confluences of sacred rivers, a snow-bound cave in Kashmir, the sea-shore at India's southernmost tip, where there is nothing ahead save sea and sky. There are the Charon Dham (the Four Heavens), at the four cardinal points; Jagannath Puri to the east, Rameshwaram in the extreme south, Dwarkaji on the tip of the 'elephant's ear' on the west coast, Badrinath among the eternal snows of the north. There are the Seven Sacred Rivers, and the Seven Puris; Ayodhya, Mathura, Hardwar, Ujjain, Dwarka, Jagannath and Kashi (Benares). There are the twelve Jyotir, linga temples, and the four Kumbh Melas, the bathing festivals held every three years at Prayag (Allahabad), Hardwar, Nasik and Ujjain in turn, making a complete cycle of twelve years. There are pilgrimages, like those described in this book, which involve a walk of several hundred miles and occupy anything up to three months, and like that which traverses the length of the Narmada river on one bank and back again to the starting point by way of the other bank, a matter of close on 2,000 miles on foot, occupying not less than three years. The whole of India, in one sense, is a holy land.

There is one portion however, named Uttarkhand (northern district), which through the centuries has been regarded as the special dwelling-place of the gods. It is entered through Hardwar ('the Door of Vishnu'), which is situated in the gap through which the Ganges emerges from the Himalayas onto the plains. Here is the gateway to that section of the Himalayas which includes the sources of the Ganges at Gangotri, Kedarnath and Badrinath, and the source of the Jumna at Jamnotri, all of which are little short of 200 miles from a railway.

Nowhere in the world, in an area of similar size, are found larger numbers of majestic snow-clad mountain peaks than in Uttarkhand, the northern half of the Garhwal District. Here is Nanda Devi, 25,661 feet above sea level, and Kamet, almost its equal at 25,443 feet. In a tract 30 miles long and 26 miles wide, which includes Nanda Devi, Badrinath and Kedarnath, there are four mountains over 23,000 feet, and 20 more over 21,000 feet; to east and west, not far distant, there are other great groups.

This district of unsurpassed grandeur, has been well named 'the Holy Land of the Hindus'. The ancient Vedic religion, whose gods were idealisations of the powers of Nature, recognised the mighty mountains and deep valleys of Garhwal as a fitting place for worship. Legend and history have connected this corner of the world with many famous deities, demi-gods, saints, sages, poets and philosophers who are honoured in India. The towering peaks, solitude and silence bore witness to the power and majesty of the Creator, attracting those who wished to escape from the distractions of the world and to search for the realisation of God. For centuries *sadhus* – men dedicated to the contemplative life – have sought here quiet places for retirement; religious leaders have established monasteries and trained their disciples. Here too, according to tradition, the Hindu scriptures were compiled.

This land is the magnet which draws pilgrims from their homes in every corner of India. From some date in April, when a telegraphic message from the High Priest announces that the Badrinath temple has been re-opened after its winter blockade of snow, until November when snow again closes the route, thousands of pilgrims stream along the road. In a normal year they number thirty to fifty thousand; every twelfth year, when there is a Kumbh Mela at Hardwar, there may be twice as many.

The purpose of the pilgrimage is 'release', the freeing of the soul from the bondage of its finite selfhood, its salvation from ignorance and darkness. For the philosophic type of Hindu this is a metaphysical thing, but he recognises that souls may be at different stages of development; he never quarrels with those who spiritually worship a personal God, nor with those who assist their apprehension with aids to devotion such as images and pilgrimage. Hinduism never judges these practices to be false; it judges them to be appropriate to the lower levels, and it is very tender towards those levels. It is even probable that eleven centuries ago, when the main shrines of this Himalayan pilgrimage were crumbling with neglect, they were restored and the pilgrimage revived by the great Shankaracharya himself, the greatest of the Hindu philosophers of *advaita* (non-duality).

Hinduism has thus encouraged the tradition of the special sanctity of certain places. Part of the appeal of such places, in so far as it is truly religious, is *darshan*, the vision of the divinity, aided by the sensual sight of the idol which in every temple symbolises the divine presence. There is in pilgrimage also the element of *tapas*, austerity, the puritanic element latent in all religions. A pilgrimage in India, if made on foot as the scriptures enjoin, is certainly austere, even if modern transport is used to abridge its toils to some extent.

Another concept closely linked with the purpose and spirit of the pilgrimage is *tirtha*, a word which covers such a wide meaning that it cannot be expressed in any single English word. The Hindu scriptures give three kinds of *tirtha*. First there is *jangam tirtha*, living moving objects worthy of reverence; a Brahmin, a saint, a *sadhu*, a *mahatma*. Second, there is *manasa tirtha*, mental objects to be revered; mercy, forgiveness, contentment and many others, of which the highest is perfect purity of mind. Third, there is *sthawar tirtha*, fixed sacred places such as Benares (Varanasi), Hardwar and hundreds of others. In the pilgrimage to the source of the Ganges the third kind of *tirtha* naturally predominates, but the first and second ideas are inextricably interwoven with it and must never be overlooked.

The special devotion evoked by this pilgrimage is partly due to the religious appeal of two great natural wonders, the Ganges, and the Himalayas.

First, the Ganges

All religions tend to give sanctity to water; water gives physical purity, religion seeks spiritual purity, and the one is seen as a symbol of the other. Of all waters, rivers are most sacred; the flow of their water makes them appear living, their power to cleanse is more apparent, and the food by which men live is largely their gift. The great Ganges, fed by the melting of the Himalayan snows, brings plenty to the fields beside her. Little wonder that she is Ganga Mai, Mother Ganges, in the reverence of all that dwell on her banks. Little wonder either that the fame of her and the love of her have spread to the farthest confines of India, so that for millions who have never seen her she is the river, the gift of the gods for the life and the cleansing of men. There are many sacred pools, well over a thousand miles from her banks, whose waters are reputed to be, by miracle, true Ganges water, with the same power to cleanse and bless.

No-one who has seen that noble stream, big with the gifts of many tributaries, wending her cool way through the torrid plains of North India, can fail to feel something of the impulse that makes India hold her sacred. Her source then must be specially sacred, for if she is a divine gift, then her source is a place where heaven touches earth in blessing.

Three springs are held in special honour as sources of the Ganges, and two other causes contribute to make the upper waters of the river a sacred place. One is the number of *prayags*, confluences, where two streams of fairly equal size unite. It is not difficult to see why a *prayag* should be sacred to a nation where the popular mind broods on the mystery of unity and multiplicity. At a *prayag* two beings become one; the two-in-oneness is dramatised when the two are of different colours, and in the united stream the two separate strands of colour can be seen for some distance. *Prayags* are naturally more common near the source of a river, and in the upper reaches of the Ganges there are no less than five, some of which show the mingling strands of separate colour. Bathing at these *prayags* is considered an act of piety of great merit.

The second factor that increases the sanctity of the pilgrimage to the source of the Ganges is the Himalayas from which they spring. The religious spirit has always and everywhere felt the appeal of the 'high places'; in India, wherever there are hills at all, a temple is generally on a summit. The great 'high place' for all India is the Himalayan range, the largest and finest mountain range in all the world. Imagine the feelings of a traveller as he raises his eyes from the torrid plain and sees that great line of glistening peaks. Then, as he penetrates the awesome gorges, sees something of the terrific forces of storm and snow that surge among the summits, hears the thunder of the avalanche and gazes on the towering cliffs of rock and ice, little wonder that he feels that here is the home of the gods themselves. True, the religious imagination of India has selected as the actual sacred mountain where the gods dwell, Mount Kailasa, an exceptionally lovely rounded peak not unlike a great *lingam*, 22,028 feet high, which rises 120 miles to the east in Tibet, where Europeans may not go. Thus the utmost sanctity of the Himalayas is elsewhere than at the sources, but the fact that the sources are in the sacred range, and not so far from Kailasa itself, increases their sanctity and power, so that they have become the goal of the greatest of Hindu pilgrimages.

CHAPTER 3

The Framework of the Pilgrimage

Bhishma continued: 'Listen to me as I tell you what those sacred *tirthas* are that are situated on earth. Just as the purity of conduct that I have mentioned is said to be the *tirtha* of the body, so there are particular spots on earth, and particular waters, which are considered sacred. As strength without exertion, or exertion without strength, can do nothing, and both combined can do all things, so one gifted with the purity granted by the *tirthas* in the body, and also with that granted by the *tirthas* on the earth, becomes truly pure. That purity which is derived from both sources is the best.'
(Mahabharata, Anushasana Parva, Chap. 108, 12-21.)

IT IS NOW IMPORTANT to consider the material conditions of the pilgrimage, and the framework of organisation which enables these thousands of pilgrims to accomplish their purpose. How is it all done?

1. The Route

It is essential for understanding to follow the road on the map at the end of this book. The route is at first among the foothills and later among the great peaks themselves. Kedarnath temple is reached at 11,500 feet, but Kedarnath peak which overshadows it rises to 22,853 feet. At Badrinath the route reaches 10,400 feet, and not far away is the pointed peak of Nalikanta, 21,713 feet. Beyond Vishnuprayag the road is 'outside' the 'inner line',* and to

---

* Movement of 'outsiders' in the zone immediately inside the mountainous international frontier of India on the north and northeast is controlled by Government.

9

Kedarnath Temple.

Badrinath Temple.

go beyond it Europeans are obliged to have a special permit, granted for a small fee and a written undertaking not to attempt to enter Tibet. The high parts of this land contain some of the most beautiful scenery and finest mountaineering country in the world. The lower parts are gorge and forest-clad hill, interspersed, wherever the hillmen's ingenuity has made it possible, by patches of fields, narrow, terraced strips, growing wheat and potatoes.

When I first became a pilgrim the road was a hill-track, passable only for foot-passengers and pack-animals. In view of the hosts of pilgrims the Government engineers aimed at providing a track 10 feet wide, and except in some difficult places this has been done. Landslides create difficulties, and such landslides, over a breadth of as much as two or three hundred yards, are common. The mountainside breaks away, and a section of the road has to be reconstructed at a higher level. This may happen time after time at the same place; at one place we counted traces of five such roads one above another. Other difficult places are made safer and easier by rock steps and parapets. At one point the path has been quarried out of the face of a sheer cliff for about a quarter of a mile, to a breadth and height of eight feet; this saves the pilgrim a stiff climb of two extra miles.

Along the route there are at least 17 suspension bridges, some of 80 or 90 yards span; the longest is Lachhman Jhula, 150 yards.

Lachhman Jhula, the new bridge opened in 1930.

There are many smaller bridges, and all these save the pilgrim a long detour and the hazards of the local rope bridges. By 1948 there was a motor road from Kotdwara on the plains through Pauri and Srinagar to Nandprayag, and another from Hardwar to Srinagar.

2. The Sources

Ascending the Ganges from Hardwar, one reaches the first confluence, Devaprayag. Above that the name Ganges, or Ganga, is not used. The two streams that unite here are the Bhagirathi and the Alaknanda. Some pilgrims follow the Bhagirathi northward to the famous shrine of Gangotri* ('the Descent of Ganga'); a very few go further, undertaking a difficult and dangerous two-day march to Gaomukh ('the Cow's Mouth'), the glacier cave from which the Bhagirathi river gushes out. They then return some distance down the valley, and cross the hills to Trijugi Narayan and Kedarnath. This route to Gangotri is in Tehri State, and provision for pilgrims was then scantier than in the Garhwal district of what at that time was called 'British India'.

The majority of pilgrims choose the Alaknanda valley, and follow it up to Rudraprayag, where the River Mandakini joins. Here too a choice must be made. Up the Mandakini valley is the route to Kedarnath; many pilgrims go first to Kedarnath, visiting Trijugi Narayan also, and then returning to the Alaknanda valley by the Chobta pass, and so up to Badrinath. At Badrinath there is a hot spring, and it is therefore an inevitable spot for a holy place. Like Gangotri, it is not near the actual source of the river, and the path to the source is very faint and little used.

3. The Temples

The temples on the pilgrim route are not large; even the two major ones at Badrinath and Kedarnath are not larger than is usual in a north Indian pilgrim town, and they are somewhat overshadowed by the *prayags* and sundry other places. Still, they have their importance, and some understanding of them is necessary for an understanding of the pilgrimage.

---

* The Bhagirathi is named from the royal saint Bhagirath, who is said to have obtained from the gods the boon of the descent of the Ganges to earth. It is also said that the god Shiva, in the form of a naked ascetic, received her waters on his head.

Think of the temple as a palace in which the god dwells, as a great (Indian) Rajah dwells in his palace. He is woken in the morning by music, is washed and fed; he retires for his siesta, and emerges with music in the evening. Most of the ritual of a Hindu temple can be thus understood; it is a court meeting the daily needs of its king. The Hindu Rajah invariably gives something in return; he is expected to be daily accessible to his people, receiving their homage, hearing their complaints, dispensing justice. In the same way, at certain hours the idol is visible to all comers, and sits to receive their worship, not the worship of a congregation in a mass meeting, but the homage of individuals and groups as they happen to come. The idol, the stone or metal image, is the centre of attention.

There are two main Hindu sects, the Vaishnavites or devotees of Vishnu, and the Shaivites, the devotees of Shiva. For the Vaishnavites Vishnu is the true God Almighty, of whom all other gods are aspects or minor companions. In a Vaishnavite temple the idol is in human form, representing Vishnu himself under one or other of his titles, or some closely associated deity. In a temple with such a human idol, the parallel with the rajah is easy to see. The Shaivites regard Shiva as the High God. By a process of cult-mingling lost in the mists of antiquity they place in their temples not a human image, but a highly stylised representation of the organs of generation, a symbol of the creative and life-giving power of God. This object of worship is called the *lingam*; with this image, the full rajah-ceremonial of the Vaishnavites would not be appropriate. The general pattern of worship however is similar. There is the regular ceremonial performed by temple priests, and the more occasional but still ceremonial homage of the individuals and groups who visit the shrine.

For both sects the essence of worship is *darshan*, gift and prayer. There is no altar, no sacrifice; the gods are as vegetarian as their high-caste worshippers, and accept the gift of symbolic grain and flowers. All shrines, Vaishnavite and Shaivite, are open to all caste Hindus, and though the Shaivite pilgrim values most highly the *darshan* of Shiva at Kedarnath, and the Vaishnavite that of Vishnu at Badrinath, nearly all pilgrims go to both.

The temple building is suited to this form of worship. There is an inner chamber containing the idol, over which a great tower is built. In front of this inner chamber is an entrance-hall, large enough to accommodate a band of musicians when needful. That is all there is of the temple proper, but it is often surrounded by an enclosed courtyard containing the kitchens for cooking the sacred food, store-rooms, and a tank for ritual bathing if there is no river close by. Precautions are taken to avoid ceremonial pollution of the idol, and one has to ascertain locally how far a non-Hindu may go; answers may vary from person to person or from time to time.

The Chief Priest of an important temple is a potentate who often controls vast wealth, being a trustee for the temple properties and the munificent gifts of noble devotees. The Rawal Sahib (High Priest) of the Badrinath temple, and those of Kedarnath and Gopeshwar, are nobles. They are invariably Nambudri Brahmins, members of that sub-caste in far Travancore to which the great philosopher-restorer of these temples, Shri Shankaracharya, belonged. During the winter each lives in a palace below the snow line, and ascends to his main temple to open it and live there for the pilgrim season. Because of past mismanagement, however, the Government now requires temple finances to be managed by the civil powers of the area through a resident secretary, while the Rawal Sahib retains his traditional status and duties.

4. The *Coolies*

The *coolie*, the human carrier of loads, is quite indispensable on the pilgrimage, not only for his services as a carrier but also for his knowledge of the route. The *coolies* are one's almost constant companions, and bulk large in the pilgrim life.

Coolies are engaged through a contractor at Muni Ki Reti near Rishikesh, in the territory of Tehri State to which most of them belong. A written contract is made, of which the contractor, the *coolie* and the pilgrim each keep a copy. The pay depends partly on the route planned, and partly on the current price of wheat. In 1923 the rate was Rs. 75/- (then equal to £5), in 1930 it was Rs. 65/-, and in 1934 only Rs. 50/-, but since the war the figure has soared. In addition, the *coolie* is entitled to receive special gifts of money and food at Trijugi Narayan, Kedarnath and Badrinath, and half an *anna* (about three *pice*) daily for parched *gram* to chew on the road.

When the contract is made, the luggage is weighed in the presence of two of the Tehri State police. The legal limit for one man's load is eighty pounds, and since the war sixty pounds. Some pigrims shamelessly add to the weight later. The *coolies* however can obtain redress at certain checkpoints along the road, which they know and the pilgrims do not. It seems strange that people should try to cheat in this mean way, and to exploit the men on whom so much of their comfort depends, while they are actually engaged in an enterprise of religious duty, and when their scriptures warn them that 'sins committed at a sacred place leave an indelible stain and can never be removed'.

A Coolie *with a 'thin' pilgrim in a Kandi.*

Coolies will carry not only luggage but also the pilgrims themselves. There are some who by choice or from necessity travel on other men's feet. The cheapest way is in a *kandi*, a basket made of *ringal* (hill bamboo) carried on the *coolie's* back. The passengers sit as in an armchair, with a rest for their feet, and one often sees them peacefully dozing as they go. But only the thinner pilgrims can get into a *kandi*; the heavier ones have to use a *jhampan*, a string-woven seat slung on poles and carried by four *coolies*, or the more comfortable and expensive *dandi* (sedan-chair) with a hood for protection against rain. One might meet the stout merchant in charge of a party travelling in a *dandi*, his wife in another, his mother in a *jhampan*, and auntie or grannie following behind in a *kandi* with the luggage *coolies*.

Good *coolies* help one's pilgrimage immensely, and on the whole I found them very good. Most of them are fine-looking, high-caste men, Kshattriyas or even Brahmins, from poor hill villages where this supplementary source of income is much needed. One heard of a few cases of minor pilfering, but the general rule is honesty, hard work, and real loyalty and friendliness.

5. The Pilgrims

My first reason for undertaking the pilgrimage was to make friends; I spent quite half my time in chatting to people. This constant company had its tiring side, but for the most part it was a privilege and a joy. India is a land of many distinctive types and areas, and the pilgrimage was a cavalcade containing them all. It was amusing to try to guess where people came from; the colour and cut of their clothes, their speech, the way they do their *turbans*, the presence or absence of beards and the way they are trimmed; all have a meaning. One group had a beard cut that defeated us; they turned out to be Brahmins from Hoshiapur.

Most pilgrims were old or middle-aged; I should guess that about eighty percent had some grey hair. This was natural; the old can more easily retire for a while from active affairs. The sexes were about equally divided, but there were more young women than young men. Again this was natural; young men could not easily leave their affairs, and the pilgrimage attracted some young women because it was reputed to reward childless wives with sons. The number of children was negligible, except for a few very small babies carried by their mothers.

My first impression was of friendliness. With very few exceptions my fellow pilgrims were friendly and helpful, both to one another and also to me. The next impression was of the courage of the old and infirm. Many of them had never before travelled by train; few had any clothes beyond the thin cottons of the plains; some were ill, almost walking skeletons. They would be on the road long before dawn, struggle on till late morning, rest during the heat, then start again at two and keep on till dusk. In this way they kept up with the rest. A woman, one of whose legs had been amputated above the knee after an accident in a Calcutta mill, walked with a pair of bamboo crutches, with unpadded blocks under the arms; she averaged a daily march almost equal to my own. I watched a blind man, with no companion, feel his way with his two sticks along a path zigzagging down a very steep slope, edging his way round a hairpin bend. It took him about five minutes, but he did it. Other blind people were led with a stick held by a friend; they too were wonderful enough to watch. Most of the pilgrims were villagers, but among them were also a number of the educated and wealthy.

6. Health and Sanitation

A pilgrimage brings together in a most dangerous combination two important factors in Indian life – its fly-borne diseases and its traditional sanitation. Dysentery is chronic, and cholera endemic. People from many parts of India carry many disease germs, and if there is a plague of flies with access to excreta, the disease spreads.

A plague of flies there certainly is, and a great majority of the pilgrims are villagers, accustomed to relieving themselves under cover of darkness in the open fields. The habits of a lifetime are not broken on the pilgrim routes, and when each season 40,000 people practise these habits along a narrow path, the results both increase the fly nuisance and make it germ-ridden. Watercourses near the road are fouled and another menace to health is created.

The Government does its best to minimise these dangers. Resthouses are provided with piped water from far above the road, and special scavengers are attached to them. Springs are enclosed in masonry and provided with spouts. Watercourses crossing the road are fenced off. Nevertheless obstinate pilgrims circumvent the rules and break down the protective fences. Fly-borne diseases are thus common.

So are lung problems. Many pilgrims are old and very few are used to a cold climate. There are eight Government hospitals along the route and there is plenty of work for the doctors. In 1930 the doctor at Badrinath told me that during the six weeks that had passed since the opening of the road he had had reports of forty deaths along the nineteen miles between Joshimath and Badrinath. But the hospitals are not so much used as they should be. Both the *coolies* and the sick pilgrim himself fear delays, so he will not go to the hospital, or if he does go he will not stay for treatment. Indeed he is not sure that he wishes to recover, since death in such a sacred place is accounted a spiritual blessing. Patients are torn between their natural love of life and their longing for this holy death; they go to the doctor for advice but cannot bring themselves to accept his treatment.

If a real epidemic does break out Government may attempt to stop the pilgrimage, but things have to be very bad indeed before this drastic step is taken. Many people along the route depend on the pilgrimage for their living; many pilgrims are very poor, and by the time they reach Hardwar by train they have spent so much that if they were to be sent back from there they could never hope to make the pilgrimage again. On my last visit (1948) the Badrinath doctor told me that in 1939 at least a thousand pilgrims had died of cholera, and there had been ghastly scenes along the road, but even so the pilgrimage was allowed to continue.

These unpleasant facts must be included if the picture of the pilgrimage is to be a truthful one. I have written as mildly as I could, but the sickness and stench is part of the pilgrim life, along with the spiritual aspirations, the friendships and humours of the way, and the glorious mountain scenery.

7. The *Chattis* or Resthouses

The Indian villager's needs are very simple. He uses no furniture, and prefers food to be cooked by himself or his family. On pilgrimage his needs are fully met by a series of simple shelters; when these are privately owned they are called *chattis*; when they are maintained as charities to help the poor they are called *dharmashalas*. They are set at short intervals along the road, rarely more than three miles apart, wherever possible near water and shade. Most are one-storeyed buildings roofed with whatever material is locally available – grass, *ringal* stems, wood or stone. The earthen floor is plastered with a mixture of cow dung and mud, frequently renewed – hygienic and pleasant to sleep on. The only furniture is a long row of big smooth stones, placed in pairs against the back wall, which provide fireplaces for cooking. These are whitewashed after every use to preserve caste purity, but there is no outlet for the smoke, and the result is hard on those who are not used to it.

The keeper of the *chatti* has stocks of rice, wheatflour, lentils, sugar, salt, pepper and *ghee* (clarified butter), though at the far end of the road salt and pepper may be almost unobtainable. Pilgrims

Khankra Chatti.

who buy from the keeper may use the *chatti* to cook and sleep; if they do not buy from him he may demand rent, and insists on his right to do so. In some cases this may seem harsh, but the *chatti* is his livelihood, expenses are heavy and the trade only seasonal, so he cannot afford to do otherwise.

The main discomfort in the *chattis* is the flies – a terrible trial, especially at medium altitudes. When one enters, it seems as if the walls and floor rise up to meet one with the roaring buzz of innumerable wings. Anything placed on the floor immediately becomes black with flies, as does any foodstuff exposed for sale. It is both dangerous and nauseating.

8. The *Pandas*

Pandas are Brahmins who have the hereditary right of showing pilgrims the sacred places and guiding them through the rites and ceremonies. During the winter, when the pilgrim road is blocked with snow, they and their agents tour India persuading people to make the pilgrimage. The *panda* meets his customers at Hardwar and takes them through to Badrinath. There the pilgrim settles accounts. This almost invariably means haggling, until the *panda* sees that he can hope for no more; only then will he accept the pilgrim's offering and give the assurance that the pilgrimage will be 'fruitful'. As there are resident *pandas* at each sacred place, acting as local guides and charging local fees, the pilgrimage often costs more than their victims have allowed for, and many poor pilgrims are put to great anxiety. The whole business is, to put it mildly, most displeasing; many orthodox pilgrims are themselves its severest critics. But it takes great moral courage for a pilgrim to defy his Brahmin guide, and reform is far from easy.

Even we, who did not perform the ceremonials, found that *pandas* took much shaking off. However, like most of the pilgrims, we were not often troubled on the way home; when we were, the best answer was the Hindi proverb: 'there is no oil left in the oil-cake' – which is the equivalent of the English phrase about the 'squeezed lemon'.

Most of the local residents, like the *pandas*, look on the pilgrims as sheep to be fleeced. Shopkeepers raise their prices and wherever possible adulterate their goods, and beggars of all sorts abound. But beggars abound all over India, and it has to be remembered that the shopkeepers, like the *chatti*-keepers, are dependent on a seasonal trade. They behave, after all, in much the same way as do their counterparts in popular holiday resorts in other parts of the world.

9. The Charities of the Road

In contrast to this fleecing of the pilgrims, it is pleasant to record the works of genuine charity which the pilgrimage has inspired. Many of these are carried on by the followers of an ascetic known as Baba Kala Kamliwala, 'the saint with the black blanket'. His title is 'Shri 108', which means that his holiness entitled him to have the honorific 'Shri' repeated 108 times before his name. He died about the end of the last century, leaving a large following of rich merchants drawn from all over India.

This group of men maintains many charitable services along the pilgrim way. There are *dharmshalas*, free resthouses, for poor pilgrims. There are meal tickets for penniless, genuine *sadhus*, which enable them to obtain at each stage of the journey a ration of grain, lentils and *ghee*, which the shopkeeper then charges to the merchant whose name is printed on the ticket. There are blankets for loan to pilgrims who have no warm clothes. At many places along the road, where water is not naturally found, there is a little hut with a notice which reads: 'By command of Shri 108 Baba Kala Kamliwala Set A. B. of . . . has established this drinking place'. Inside the hut sits a man with some big earthenware jars of water, who supplies any and every thirsty pilgrim, and receives a salary from the merchant named. In other places, where there is no Government hospital, the Kali Kamliwalas maintain dispensaries, of which there were eight along the route.

I had many pleasant encounters with the Kali Kamliwalas, and I must record also, in all fairness, that there were occasions when even among the *pandas*, whose hereditary calling exposes them to so many temptations to callousness, I met with genuine and spontaneous kindnesses which will be described in their place.

PART II
THE 1923 PILGRIMAGE

CHAPTER 4

Initiation

'Hari Krishna, Hari Krishna, and other names of God on his tongue, and remembering Shri Hari in his heart, the wise man proceeds on his pilgrimage on foot.'

(Padma. Patal)

IT HAD BEEN MY DESIRE for several years to visit one or more of these sacred places, expecting that there I might meet with true seekers after God, men who would be prepared to give careful consideration to the teaching of Christ. In my spare time I had sought acquaintance with the *sadhu* community; had experimented with *sadhu* dress and given much thought to footwear, and in 1923 my opportunity came.

There are many well-defined styles of *sadhu's* dress, which the initiated can distinguish at a glance. I chose one often worn by *sannyasis*; it consisted of an ochre-coloured *dhoti* or loin-cloth, a roomy shirt reaching to the knee, and a *turban*, to which I added, as is allowable for a *sadhu*, an umbrella. These clothes are very comfortable and cool, and are well-suited to a life in which the 'conveniences' of so-called civilisation are left behind. The looseness of the shirt allowed me to wear underneath, at higher altitudes, a vest, waistcoat and sweater, without which I should not have been able to sleep because of the intense cold. I folded the *turban* over the crown of an old felt hat; this was sufficient protection from the sun, and the umbrella helped to protect my face. I wore a cross conspicuously round my neck, so that even those who did not speak to us should be in no doubt that I was a Christian.

Comfortable footwear is of the greatest importance. The road is rough and the rocks sharp even for those who have always walked barefoot. Various kinds of cheap canvas and rope-soled shoes are available in the villages on the route, but they are soon worn out. I had been given a pair of Kashmiri sandals; they were sturdy, but the leather was too stiff. I had them copied in softer leather, and tested them out before I started. They were very comfortable, but I was so anxious that they should last out the journey that I once used another pair, and blistered a toe so badly that it had to be bandaged for the rest of the journey, more than 200 miles, and the mark endures to this day.

My companion was an Indian Christian friend of long standing named Khushilal, who had accompanied me on other journeys and had proved his worth a hundred times. He is a man of deep

*G.W.M. and Khushilal
(wearing pectoral crosses)
with Mendar Singh,
1923.* *See p. 32.*

spiritual experience, with an attractive way of speaking and an intimate knowledge of Hindu life and thought. He not only took the lead in our conversations with other pilgrims, he also managed our domestic concerns and did the cooking for us both.

We travelled the 800 miles to Hardwar by train, arriving late at night, and slept on the waiting room floor till morning. At first light we began making enquiries about *coolies* and discovered that they are engaged at Rishikesh, fourteen miles further on. I changed into my *sadhu's* clothes at the Dak Bungalow,* and left my English ones in the charge of the caretaker. Then we drove to Rishikesh in an *ekka* – surely one of the most uncomfortable vehicles ever devised by the wit of man! Since reading *Pennell of the Afghan Frontier*, which describes his experiences as a *sadhu* in Rishikesh, I had been wanting to see the town, but as the place where *coolies* were engaged was a mile and a half further on, we did not stay. It appeared to be a prosperous place, and as we drove through it I saw for the first time the name 'Baba Kala Kamliwala' over the doorway of a new *dharmashala*.

As we turned a corner a busy scene met our eyes. Crowds of *coolies* and pilgrims were collected round a large tree, from which hung a spring balance. Two Tehri State policemen were weighing things as fast as they could. The rate was more than I had expected, and I could not afford more than one *coolie*, so we had to reduce our luggage and leave behind our tiny tent. Our *coolie* was a young man named Gopal Singh; during the six weeks he was with us he became devoted to us and was just one of the party. As the days passed we got to know many of the other *coolies*, passing and re-passing on the road as we did. They responded so cheerfully to any friendly word, and their powers of endurance were wonderful.

We spent our first night under the stars on the Ganges sand, much pleasanter than the stuffy *dharmshala*. We had several visitors; a number of *sadhus* came to ask who we were, and a dear old gentleman with a long beard, hearing that an Englishman was camping out, came to beg us to accept more comfortable quarters.

Soon after daylight we packed up. The previous day Khushilal had bought some potatoes; as he was packing he left them on the

---

* Literally, the 'mail' bungalow; a government rest house available for a small fee to the public when not required by officials.

sand for a few moments, and when he turned to pick them up again they were gone. Ten yards away sat a circle of red-faced monkeys, each solemnly munching a potato. It was nearly a fortnight before we came across potatoes again.

We were just about to start when a young man came running up to ask for medicine for a scorpion sting. At these lower altitudes the scorpions are large and virulent, and the sting is sometimes fatal. A day or two later I was again stopped by a man whose wife had been stung; she was being carried in a *kandi*, groaning with pain. I rubbed the place vigorously with crystals of potassium permanganate in a damp rag, and in a few moments the pain had almost gone. The *coolie* who had been carrying her was so impressed that he begged for my address, so that he might bring me holy water from Gaomukh – a task that would have meant weeks of difficult tramping. It was a great honour, but I explained that for me no water was more sacred than any other; that was quite a new idea for him.

A mile and a half of level road brought us to Lachhman Jhula, a fine suspension bridge. This whole area is rich in famous temples and sacred places, where *sadhus* come to meditate, and where devout Hindus come from Hardwar to bathe and worship. It is from Lachhman Jhula that the real pilgrimage begins. The pilgrim leaves 'civilisation' behind and enters a different country. On each side of the river the mountains rise steeply from the water's edge, and the narrow path ahead will never for long be out of sight of the sacred stream.

Not far above the bridge was a large temple garden, watered by a clear stream, and containing hundreds of banana trees. A rather forbidding priest was seated outside. I greeted him, and enquired whether he would be willing to sell me some bananas. 'No', he replied abruptly, 'we need all the fruit for religious purposes. And anyway, what do you a Christian want, going to Badrinath? There are no Christians there, nor likely to be!'

By ten o'clock it was getting very hot, and when we reached a *chatti* we found it packed full of pilgrims who had arrived before us, so we went a little further and found a cool shady spot by a lovely stream, where a few humble pilgrims were cooking their own food. Among them was a Gurkha soldier who was going on leave to his village among the hills, with his wife and tiny baby, who had come to meet him. Cooking next to us was a *sannyasi* from Almora, with his mother and sister, who were all dressed in the saffron cloth. We made friends with them, and we met them again and again during the following weeks. As our friendship developed we gave the *sannyasi* a gospel, which he began to read at once. At our last meeting he told me that he had been reading the book to someone else, who became so interested that he had given it to him. Had we, he now asked, another copy? He gladly bought Luke and Acts, and went on his way rejoicing.

That afternoon we stopped at the first *chatti* we came to; we had covered eleven miles and decided that that was enough, as we were not yet used to our burdens. Towards sunset the *chatti* filled up, and a number of people came and began to ask questions. Among them two men who spoke English well, one a Bengali, the other a Punjabi. The Bengali did not seem pleased to find me there, and asked rather unpleasantly whether I belonged to the Secret Service. When I told him I did not he said, 'then why are you in disguise?' 'Why do you call it a disguise when everyone can see I am a European?' Then the Punjabi joined in, 'He asks why are you in this guise, not disguise'. The Bengali at once said, 'No, I said DISGUISE', laying more emphasis on the word than before. People were gathering round, so for their benefit I asked, in Hindi, whether he had ever noticed any Indians wearing European dress. 'Would you say that they belonged to the Secret Service? or were in disguise?' The Punjabi suddenly doubled up with laughter, and the Bengali said no more. The next time I saw him he was wearing trousers and a felt hat, and I understood how my answer had gone home. I met him again several times and by the end he became quite cordial. The Punjabi apologised for the way the Bengali had spoken; we had a long talk and became great friends.

Just beyond this *chatti* the old road in the narrow gorge of the Ganges has been abandoned, as the hillside above it is so loose that it has become very dangerous. The new road turns up the Hiul valley, climbs over a high ridge, and drops steeply down to the Ganges ten miles further on. So the next morning we started on the long, weary climb over the ridge. The saddle at the top was only a few yards wide; it seemed as if one could almost have thrown a stone into a strip of Ganges water visible 3,000 feet below. By the time we reached a *chatti* it was hot, but the *chatti* was not attractive and we decided to go on to the next, three miles further on. That did not seem much, as it was all downhill, but we soon regretted our decision. Our unaccustomed knees gave way on the steep descent; the mountainside, facing the sun, became burning hot, and Gopal Singh, barefoot as he was, walked like a cat on hot bricks. I gave him the shoes I was wearing, and found another pair for myself. 'The *sahib* has given me back my life', said he gratefully as he put them on.

Not long afterwards, as I went ahead, I heard a crash and a clanging of metal. Turning round, I saw that Khushilal's bundle had burst, and that the circular brass box, whose lid and bottom were our plate and saucepan, was merrily bumping down the mountainside, scattering pepper pot, salt tin and assortment of vital things, with apparently no reason for stopping till it reached the Ganges far below. We held our breath and watched it gather momentum, but presently it caught on a bush and came to rest. The tension over, we sat down and laughed heartily. If it had gone, it would have been no laughing matter.

When there was still half a mile to go to reach the next *chatti*, we came to shade and water; we were so tired and thirsty that we stopped to cook our midday meal there, and a few other belated pilgrims did the same. One woman arrived with the news that a little *coolie* boy with a heavy load was lagging behind, crying with the pain of his burned and swollen feet. Leaving Khushilal with the cooking I went back to look for him. I thought he was a boy I already knew by sight, and I found him and helped him along, only to find I had brought in the wrong boy!

We were soon talking with the whole party, who sat round as freely as if I had been an Indian – in fact I don't think that they thought of me as anything else. When we finally moved on to the *chatti* there was no space, but our Punjabi friend was there and greeted us, and very soon the occupants moved off for their afternoon march, leaving us in peace.

Next day we were both painfully stiff. I have never known such stiffness. It was agony to take even a few steps on the down grade. But in two or three days it had worn off and along with it had disappeared the feeling of strangeness on the road.

Devaprayag to Rudra Prayag

Devaprayag is the first of the five great confluences, where the Bhagirathi river meets the Alaknanda. It is from this point that the river officially becomes known as the Ganges. Here the road divides; one branch following the Bhagirathi river to Gangotri and beyond to Gaomukh, the traditional source of the Ganges, where according to the sacred books, the goddess Ganges descended upon the matted locks of the god Shiva as he was engaged in meditation. The other road follows the Alaknanda to Badrinath, the one that is followed by the majority of pilgrims.

Devaprayag is the headquarters of the *panda* community. There are no *chattis* as it is assumed that all pilgrims will stay at their respective *panda's* houses. Accommodation is difficult for those who have no *panda*. A large *dharmshala* is available, but on this occasion it was already full, and in any case dirty and unattractive. We would have fared badly if the Brahmin postmaster had not come to the rescue and offered us the hospitality of his own house. I was able to repay a little of his kindness by helping him compose answers to some official correspondence that had been beyond his attainments in English.

On the steep promontory between the two rivers stands a temple sacred to Ramchandraji. Ramchandraji is said to have passed a thousand years here in purification after killing the ten-headed Ravana, the demon king of Ceylon. Inside the temple is a six-foot black stone idol of Ramchandraji, but the *sinhasan* or throne is kept outside. The idol is ancient and said to have been established by Shri Shankaracharya. The doorkeeper takes one *pice* from every worshipper.

The bathing *ghat* at the confluence is a cheerful sight in the bright sunlight. Women pilgrims put on their best and brightest clothing after bathing, just for the day. It is a natural bathing *ghat*; great slabs of shelving rock go down to a point at the junction where the water races past on either side. Strong iron chains are fastened to the rock to hang onto so as not to get swept away. Even so accidents occur. A flagstaff marks the place where the waters mingle and pilgrims try to take their dip as near as possible to that point. After the bathe men pilgrims' heads are shaved before the important ceremony of *pind shraddh*, the obligation offered to the spirits of departed ancestors. Little marble-sized balls of wholemeal flour are made for each relative and thrown into the river, where shoals of sacred fish, fat on previous offerings, wait in a swirling mass, to gulp them down.

After leaving Devaprayag and passing through Bilwakedar, the confluence of the Khandawa river with the Alaknanda, the path runs close beside the water and there is a convenient bathing place with plenty of room for everyone. We took the opportunity to bathe and wash some clothes, which soon dried on the warm rocks.

Approaching Srinagar, the chief town of Garhwal, there was a crowd of ragged children lying in wait for the pilgrims. They danced along a step or two in front of their intended victims, whirling round and round, chanting songs about sacred places and begging for money. It only makes matters worse to give them anything, as they have eyes at the back of their heads and know immediately if anything has been given!

At Srinagar we found several Christians connected with the American Methodist Episcopal Mission. We arrived in the evening in a violent dust storm, the prelude to a heavy shower, and were warmly welcomed by the Indian pastor.

Srinagar, though about 75 miles from Hardwar, is only 1,749 feet above sea level and is extremely hot in summer. During our stay we visited the famous Kamaleshwar temple, the only building to survive the Gohna flood disaster of 1894. The previous year, a small tributary of the Alaknanda, 60 miles further upstream, had been blocked by a huge landslide, filling up the valley for three miles. A lake began to form, and it was foreseen that when the lake filled and broke the natural dam, there would be a terrific flood. Telegraphic communication was established and the valley inhabitants warned and prepared for flight. The lake filled to a depth of 700 feet before giving way. The telegraph flashed the news all down the valley and the people fled to safety. The huge volume of water swept everything before it, but on account of the preparations very few lives were lost. At Karnprayag, the sacred place at the junction of the Pindar river with the Alaknanda, where the river takes a right-angled turn, the water piled up to a height of 160 feet. At Srinagar, where the valley is widest, the water rose 100 feet owing to a curve further down. There is still a beautiful lake left, two miles long, half a mile wide and 300 feet deep, some distance off the pilgrim track.

The night after leaving Srinagar we stayed at Khankra *chatti*, where a large number of pilgrims had arrived. We had barely finished supper when a heavy thunderstorm came on. The *chatti* keeper peremptorily gave the order to extinguish all fires, which those still cooking were slow to obey. The reason for the order became apparent when a sudden gust of wind swirled in at the open front of the *chatti*, scattering glowing pieces of wood in all directions. These were speedily dealt with and no harm done; but it was easy to see that carelessness might have serious results, as pilgrim's clothing or belongings, or *chatti* roofs might catch fire and the damage be irreparable. Rain continued all night. We had to shift our position several times to avoid the drips. In the morning the temperature had dropped to 50°F; by midday it was as hot as ever.

Rudraprayag to Trijugi Narayan

Seventeen miles from Srinagar is another junction, Rudraprayag, where the Mandakini river joins the Alaknanda. In 1922 the American Methodist Mission opened a little school. In charge was a young schoolmaster, living with his parents, the father being an evangelist. We had a very happy time with them and stayed overnight. The whole district for 10 miles around is terrorised by a man-eating leopard. He has been at large for six years and is so cunning that all efforts to kill him have so far failed. The inhabitants are inclined to be superstitious, so do not help the huntsmen, and will give no information for fear of bringing bad luck if they were the means of his death. When he kills, which may be as often as once a week, he eats to repletion, but never comes back to the kill, and is probably next heard of 10 or 15 miles away. The Deputy Commissioner told me that on one occasion the leopard stole into an upper room, where a whole family was sleeping and seized the man by the throat and dragged him out by the door. The wife woke and grasped the man's feet and screamed for help. Neighbours came and made a great noise, and the leopard left leaving his victim dead and escaped in the darkness. While the people were still gathered comforting the wife, the leopard killed again at the other end of the village.

On our way back some weeks later we were told the leopard had that very day been run to earth and the mouth of the cave where he had taken refuge blocked up with stones. On the strength of this report we decided to sleep out of doors. We were not the only visitors this time at the Mission – a school master from Headquarters had come to inspect the school. Khushilal and I were pretty skinny by that time, and the school master was the reverse. Though he agreed to sleep out with us, he was plainly ill at ease, and barricaded himself in, with me on his open side. After suggesting, to cheer him up, that a leopard or tiger invariably selected the plumpest of the party, I wished him goodnight. We later heard that the leopard had not been trapped after all.

[NOTE: The leopard seemed to have a charmed life and was not disposed of until three years later, by which time it had killed 125 people, 26 of whom were claimed in the year we were there. It was eventually killed by Jim Corbett, the famous tiger and leopard hunter, after many months of fruitless effort. Its story has been written by Jim Corbett in *The Man-Eating Leopard of Rudraprayag*. In the end it was killed on the pilgrim road at Gulabrai *chatti*, about a mile from Rudraprayag. In an article in the Allahabad *Pioneer*, dated 15 May, 1926, it says: 'The career of the animal makes one of the strangest of the many strange stories told of the Himalayas, so strange indeed, that it might be doubted if the details, many of them tragic and gruesome, were not so well established'.]

At Rudraprayag we engaged another *coolie*, as we were finding the carrying of our loads too exhausting, and knew the worst part of the journey was still ahead of us. We made a happy choice in Mendar Singh, who could scarcely speak any Hindi, but had many loveable characteristics, and turned out to be a very good worker. His home was some distance from Rudraprayag, and he had only come in to do some shopping when he met us and agreed to come with us. I asked him how his wife would find out what had happened to him. He replied, that when he didn't return, she would probably assume that the leopard had got him. His neighbours would then send out a search party and make enquiries, and when they got to Rudraprayag the shopkeeper would inform them that he had gone on pilgrimage and would turn up again safe and sound in a month's time.

The Mandakini river, beside which the road to Kedarnath now passes, is clear and transparent in contrast to the Alaknanda, which in some lights appears opaque olive green. Below the junction at Rudraprayag the two colours can be seen side by side for some

distance down the river. The Mandakini valley is rich in archaeo-
logical interest. Wide and level, the valley appears to have been the
bed of a lake at one time. Thirteen miles further on Guptkashi is
reached, a comparatively large village with a famous old temple. In
the courtyard is a sacred pool, into which two springs run, one issuing from a carved stone cow's mouth; the other from an elephant's.
The water from one is said to come from the Ganges; the other
from the Jumna. The village is long and straggling, but commands
fine views up the valley to the mighty glistening peaks of Kedarnath.

The search for wild yellow raspberries – a rare treat to find fresh
fruit – had delayed our arrival at Guptkashi, where a large crowd
of pilgrims had gathered. They had already secured accommodation for the night, and we had difficulty in finding a room. The
reason why so many pilgrims aim to spend the night there, is that
the vision of the god in the temple and bathing in the sacred pool,
are said to destroy even the most heinous sins.

At Nala, a short distance further on, there is another ancient
temple dating from the time of Shankaracharya (8th century). Here
the attendant was calling the pilgrims to 'come and see the 330
million gods'. Khushilal was anxious to accept the invitation, but
I was sure there was a catch somewhere and that we would only be
pestered for money. So Khushilal went in alone. Presently he came
out with every sign of disgust written on his face. The attendant
had asked him which particular god he wanted to see, expecting
Khushilal to name his own particular deity, then he would produce
something said to be the one required. Khushilal insisted he had
been invited to see the whole lot at once, and would be content
with no less. As neither would give way, Khushilal left disappointed.
Nearby at Bhenta there are said to be 300 temples; most being only
two or three feet high. Only a few of the larger ones now contain
images, and many have fallen into disrepair. These also are said to
belong to the time of Shankaracharya.

At a turn in the road we suddenly came across a little party of
Tibetan traders. They were taking goods up to Trijugi Narayan and
giving their pack animals a rest during the heat of the day, while
refreshing themselves with a cup of tea. It looked rather an unap-
petizing mixture in greasy wooden bowls, and on enquiring I
found that instead of milk and sugar it was their custom to use salt
and clarified butter. They knew just enough Hindi to carry on a

conversation and enquired what I had slung over my shoulder. On discovering it was my violin, they wanted me to play it. We sang them a Hindi hymn, which they enjoyed, and I suggested that as we had sung to please them, they should allow me to take their photograph, which they smilingly agreed to.

In many places by the roadside there are little shrines, built of rough stone, varying in height, containing images of various gods and goddesses. The guardians, usually Brahman men or boys, urge passers-by to approach and view the god. Most pilgrims heed the call on the principle of not missing any opportunity of acquiring merit, or of avoiding the risk of offending any deity. So they approach, stand on one foot, joining the palms of their hands, and raising them to their foreheads as they bow. Then they offer a small coin and in return receive a spoonful of Ganges water with an assurance of the blessing. The guardians of these shrines usually admitted to us that it was a way of earning a living and had little religious significance.

One day I was accosted by a small boy, who was guarding an idol without any pretence of a shrine. He followed me a long way, repeating his begging formula over and over again, until I grew weary of his whine, and I had to think of some way to escape. First I quickened my pace, but he broke into a trot to keep up. At last I thought of addressing him in English, and being tired, started counting as fast and as expressively as I could. The device was immediately successful; before I had reached 60 he had disappeared round the corner and did not return.

Three miles off the road to Kedarnath, on a high ridge, is the sacred place of Trijugi Narayan. It involves a stiff climb, but the cool air and scenery are enough reward. As we were going up we met our Punjabi friend, whom we had not seen for several days, coming down. I told him that had it not been for the snowy peaks in the distance, I felt I could be in England. The trees, the flowers, the butterflies were all English. Overhead horse chestnuts were in full bloom; bushes of white wild roses, and on the ground dog violets, wild strawberry flowers in abundance, buttercups and marsh marigolds. Above them hovered small tortoiseshells, painted ladies, fritillaries, and small blues. I could only dawdle along not wanting to miss the smallest detail.

Nearby the temple in Trijugi Narayan is another building in which a fire is perpetually burning, and had been burning for many ages. Devout pilgrims leave money to buy wood to sustain it. It is here that the marriage of the god Shiva and the goddess Parvati is said to have taken place.

We stayed in the *dharmshala* here which was not overcrowded. I went out walking, but heavy rain came on, and it seemed gloomy without the sunshine. I found two blooms of single white peonies, and realised that the woods must have been a wonderful sight a week or so earlier. I also found a bush of deep pink wild roses, and the white rose was in full bloom – a lovely sight.

That evening a *sadhu* of the Ram Krishna Mission expounded his beliefs at great length. He seemed so entirely satisfied that I did not feel it was any use to do more than listen and try and understand his point of view for the benefit of my own education.

Of our two neighbours that night, one was a *sadhu* with a huge ulcer on a badly swollen foot. He was in dire need of antiseptics and clean bandages; too much for us to tackle. The other was also a *sadhu*, whom we had been meeting for some days. He had a cough. Until then I had not realised that a cough held such possibilities, nor that there was a characteristic Indian cough, distinct from the European. Owing to the climate and altitude, coughs and colds are common, and I had not lived with the Indian variety so intimately before. There was evidently something tickling this poor man right in the innermost recesses of his lungs, and he was determined not to be beaten by it. It seemed to elude him though; just out of reach. I was awake most of the night and so was Gopal Singh, as after an especially violent paroxysm, I could hear chuckles from his direction. Sometimes I feared for the man's life, but he survived to meet us many times along the road.

Pilgrims who have been to Jamnotri and Gangotri join those going to Kedarnath at Trijugi Narayan. We met a young man and his mother from Madras who had come that way, and they seemed pleased to meet us, as the young man knew about Christians in South India. Later we were able to do them a good turn, when at one of the coldest places on the road, they became separated from their *coolies* and had no blankets.

We were always on the lookout for pilgrims from our home area, and were delighted when a village schoolmaster, his wife and the school *chaprasin* settled down in the *chatti* with us. Their clothes gave them away and we hailed them as acquaintances at once. Another time, we were talking to friends whom we had not seen for some time, when a woman came up and stopped to listen to our conversation. Presently she said, 'From hearing you talk you must come from Hoshangabad District.' She came from a nearby district, but it surprised us that our way of speaking was sufficiently distinct for her to guess so accurately.

Trijugi Narayan to Kedarnath

From Trijugi Narayan the road descends steeply again to the Mandakini river. From there the road is much steeper and often very narrow. Pilgrims have to be careful, standing still sometimes to let others pass – a false step could mean certain death. It amazed me that old men and women did not seem to get dizzy at these places; yet a number of lives are lost here every year. These elderly pilgrims go on resolutely day after day, borne up by the hope of the vision and the promise of sins forgiven.

At Gaurikund, sacred because it is said to be the birthplace of Shiva's consort, Parbati, there are two bathing tanks, one of tepid water; the other a hot spring. The temperature of the former was about 70°F and the latter, which I tested twice, is 120°F. As it comes out of the brass cow's mouth into the tank it is 127°F. The river water nearby is only 46°F. The pilgrim walks down a short flight of steps into the waist-high water of the cooler tank, dips under it, and then goes to the Brahman to pay and get a mark on his forehead, before leaving the tank on the opposite side. With their wet clothes clinging to them they hurry along to the hot tank. Those courageous enough to step down and dip under, come up gasping for breath!

While we were staying here we had some interesting visitors; two *sadhus*, one young and well educated, and an older man who had been a teacher in a mission school. They brought along with them a retired doctor, who intended to spend his remaining years in meditation, and was looking for a suitable place to settle down. The doctor frankly disbelieved in the pilgrimage, recognising it for what it really is. We were beginning to reach an understanding, but reluctantly had to move on. We met them once more, as we were toiling up the last heart-breaking mile to Badrinath and they were starting back down with no chance for further talk.

A short march brought us to Rambara, from which we were to attack Kedarnath. There is a large number of *chattis* here, as pilgrims going and returning have to be accommodated. In several places the valley was blocked with snow, and the thundering river disappears under it and bursts out lower down. Eight of the *chattis* were still buried under the snow.

Where the wood used for cooking is *chhir* pine (similar to a Scots pine), it smells fragrant and the smoke not unpleasant. But at Rambara, the wood used produces a painfully acrid smoke. While the evening meal was being cooked, rain was pouring down, and the normally open front of the *chatti* was closed by matting against the cold, so the smoke of 40 cooking fires could not escape. Hindus who habitually cook on open fires are used to it, but I found it excruciating. Shutting my eyes only seemed to shut the pain in. Finally I had to lie flat on the floor, cover my face with my tear-soaked handkerchief till I gradually recovered.

It was a glorious clear morning as we started for Kedarnath at 5 a.m. Leaving Rambara we were above the tree-line and the vegetation was just beginning to recover after the melting of the snow. The mountainsides sparkled with streams of water, gay with yellow kingcups, wild iris just coming into bloom in marshy areas, and mauve and white anemones in the drier warmer places. Three hours of stiff climbing brought us out on a ridge where the road takes a sudden turn bringing us face to face with the range of 22-23,000 feet glistening peaks which we had seen several times from afar. A mile away, the temple stood at the head of the valley with this magnificent backdrop of 11,000 feet snow-covered mountains. As we approached, clouds quickly formed and the highest peaks were hidden.

> The temple ranks among the twelve famous linga shrines of India. The sanctity of the Siva linga is extolled in the Vamana Purana. Parbati asks, 'What is Kedar? What are the fruits of visiting its sacred places and bathing in its waters?' Siva replies, 'The place that you have spoken of, O goddess, is so dear to me that I shall never forsake it. When I created the universe, Kedar so pleased me that it shall ever remain sacred to me. Brahma and the other gods are there. Whoever dies there becomes one with Siva'.
>
> (Encyclopaedia of Religion and Ethics)

When we had passed up the village street to the temple we found a surprising number of pilgrims already there. The long vestibule of the temple, leading up to the tower under which the god is enthroned, was packed with worshippers, while many more waited outside. There must have been 300 altogether. Considering the inaccessibility of the place, and that the next day there will be a similar number, and so on for weeks or months, you begin to realise the large number of devotees who visit the shrines.

One of the priests came to find out who I was. He showed me the visitors book in which European, American and English speaking Indians had written their comments. Over the last 15 years or so, less than a score of foreigners had signed the book. The priest promised me a conducted tour once the crowd had left, so I wandered off to see some other sights. The ground around the village is extraordinarily spongy, like walking on sorbo rubber. Sometimes it supports one's weight, at others gives way, and one sinks up to the knees. The adhering mud is soon washed off in the next icy cold streamlet waded through. I reached a little spring a quarter of a mile outside the village. The water is perfectly clear and every few seconds gas bubbles up and explodes with a pop, said to exclaim 'Bom, Mahadeo!'

At midday Gopal Singh and I climbed with considerable difficulty up to a little frozen lake more than a mile beyond the village. There was no path and the steep side was a mass of huge boulders. Our scrambling set small rocks rolling down from above. On reaching the ridge we looked into a long narrow valley, filled with pure white snow. Just below us the little lake looked almost black in contrast. Even today devotees who wish to make the supreme sacrifice, wander off into such snowy wastes and never return. I forgot to identify the precipice from which fanatics used to jump and commit suicide. The spectacle drew large crowds, but is not permitted now.

Returning from the lake we were caught in a heavy snow storm, and found the village apparently deserted. Much to my disappointment the temple door was closed, and knowing it was the custom not to re-open till evening, I had lost the opportunity to see inside and to sign the visitors' book.

Heavy black clouds gave promise of more storms, so we hurried to start back to Rambara where we intended to spend the night so as to avoid the intense cold at Kedarnath. We met several shivering pilgrims coming up; their thin cotton clothes soaked and clinging. They looked in the depths of misery and I wondered how they would endure the night, when with our extra clothing it was hard enough to bear lower down.

A popular trophy that pilgrims carry home from this area is a stick of a thorny shrub called 'Tejbal'. It grows very straight with thorns close together. When the thorns are broken off it leaves the stick covered with excrescences reminiscent of smallpox. These are collected and ground to a powder and given to smallpox sufferers, apparently on the homoeopathic principle.

Across the Chobta Pass

From Kedarnath the pilgrims retrace their steps for 30 miles and then strike off across country, passing through Ukhimath, the winter headquarters of the High Priest of Kedarnath. There is a government hospital at Ukhimath, and the Indian doctor kindly put a small empty ward at our disposal for the day. This enabled me to develop several rolls of film, with a plentiful supply of pure spring water close at hand.

From Ukhimath we took an excursion not on the pilgrim's programme, to visit a lovely lake, Diuri Tal, situated near the summit of an 8,000 feet mountain, round which the pilgrim road winds 3,000 feet below. From there we had glorious views of some of the higher peaks, including one near Badrinath, the 22,907 feet Chaukhamba (the Four Pillars), named after the four peaks almost forming a square, like the battlements of a mighty castle. No stream enters or leaves the lake, which is a quarter of a mile long and an eighth wide. It is replenished by snow and rain. I bathed in it and enjoyed the luxury of a safe swim. Woods near the lake abound with fine trees, and rhododendrons looking like large oak trees need to be seen to be believed. We had a precipitous scramble back down to meet the road again seven miles beyond Ukhimath.

To get back again onto the main Badrinath road coming up the Alaknanda valley, we had to cross the Chobta Pass. The pass is about 9,000 feet and approached on each side by seven miles of continuous climb, and passes through the finest forest scenery of the whole trip. We were anxious to spend the night as near the top as possible, so as to visit the famous temple of Tungnath early the following morning. We continued rather later than usual, refusing the shelter of some commodious *chattis*. Hardly had we left them than the rain came on. Progress was very slow as the road became slippery. At last we saw *chattis* ahead, only to be told on reaching them that they had been booked ahead by a large party. Two smaller *chattis* were already packed to suffocation, so there was nothing for it but to accept the gentle advice to walk on to the next *chatti*. The half mile took us half an hour in the pouring rain, but we ordered a pile of wood and soon our clothes were steaming in front of a blazing pinewood fire.

Few wild animals show themselves on the busy pilgrim route. In the 14 miles of forest I saw only two pine-martens – one being chased by a crow nearly ran into me. A great variety of small, gaily plumaged birds inhabit the forests and streams of Garhwal, one of the most striking being the paradise fly-catcher; mature birds are pure white with a black head, and tail feathers twice as long as their bodies. Above 7,000 feet a kind of pheasant is found with plumage scarsely less gorgeous than the peacock's.

During the night I developed severe chest pains and difficulty in breathing. I suspected the steep climb up to Diuri Tal was responsible, and that I had a form of mountain sickness. We had intended to divert off the main route to visit Tungnath the next day. The summit at 12,000 feet is reputed to have the finest view in Garhwal, and is reached by a three mile climb from the Chobta Pass. By walking very slowly I managed to get to where the road divides. Once off the main road it soon becomes an unmaintained track and for the final mile and a half, straight up the mountain, it ceases altogether. My breathing was so painful this final part defeated me. Khushilal went on and reached the temple 500 feet below the summit, from which the view was evidently all that it was reputed to be.

I returned to the main road and followed it round to the *chattis* near where Khushilal would rejoin it later that afternoon. The pain became so bad that I could only take shallow breaths, and I lay helpless on the *chatti* floor. By afternoon I was slightly better and by going very slowly on the downhill I was able to make progress. The lower I got the better I became, and five miles further on near the bottom, I was almost right again. I never had any return of the pain even when at higher altitudes later on.

That afternoon I met some pilgrims I recognised coming up the hill, which was strange, so I spoke to them. When I had been lying down at midday, a pilgrim who had attached himself to their party had died. These men though no relative of his, had been down the hill to get wood for his cremation. They were naturally very worried by the turn of events, and I was able to advise them as to what to do with the man's effects, and make suggestions for their report to the police.

Later a young *sadhu* overtook me and we fell into conversation. He had adopted the pilgrim lifestyle purely as a way to see the world and was thoroughly enjoying himself. He had visited other sacred places, notably Amarnath in Kashmir, and thought the people there superior to the local Garhwalis. When I challenged this, he claimed the Garhwalis were sadly lacking in love. I asked him what he meant, and he told me that they were not so generous in their entertainment of *sadhus* in general and himself in particular. I hinted that as he obviously had no thought of giving anything in return, and accepted their gifts as though he was conferring a favour on them, it was not surprising that the Garhwalis were reluctant to entertain him.

At the *chatti* my young friend started a lively argument with Khushilal, which collected a crowd round us. Khushilal's bag had a leather strap and the young *sadhu* objected to the use of leather as it involved taking life. It rather weakened his argument when Khushilal pointed out that he was wearing leather shoes, much to the delight of the audience. As most of the men standing around were *kshattriyas*, and openly ate meat, as long as it did not give offence on the holy pilgrim route, the sympathy was all with Khushilal. I had another talk with the young man later. He wanted to become my disciple but finally was content to buy some Scripture portions and we parted good friends.

The next day a *sadhu* with whom we had become friendly took us to see the temple at Gopeshwar. I asked him to remember we were Christians and not take us anywhere where we would not be welcome. But the very first place he took us was the private reception room of the high priest, the holy of holies, where Christians are never admitted. The high priest realised it was a genuine mistake and was obviously relieved that no Hindus were present to witness it. He later personally showed us all that remained that we could see. The temple is dedicated to Shiva under the designation of Gopinath, the Lord of Cows. There is a local legend to the effect that a cow was grazing in the jungle, and it was noticed that its milk was falling spontaneously onto a rock having the shape of a *lingam*, the emblem of Shiva. So the spot was chosen to build a temple.

Oli Gursal

From Gopeshwar, there is a steep descent of three miles back to the Alaknanda, which is crossed by a long suspension bridge leading to the important town of Chamoli, one of the largest towns in Garhwal. There is a large, lively bazaar, several shops, post and telegraph office, law court and a hospital, but the accommodation for pilgrims is poor and always crowded as pilgrims stay at Chamoli on their way up to and back from Badrinath.

I was expecting mail so called at the Post Office. The postmaster was very agitated and implored my help. An old Hindu from South India wanted to send a telegram asking for a remittance of Rs.200. He was literally starving and no-one could be found who understood his language. It took me nearly an hour to straighten things out, and I was relieved to learn some days later that the money had been delivered to the old man on his arrival at Badrinath. The telegraph wire provided by the government has saved the lives of many pilgrims who have been fleeced by their spiritual guides.

We eventually found a corner of a verandah on the main street to rest in. We had not intended to go further that day, but the horror of the flies and nearby bazaar were too much for us and we moved in the late afternoon on to the next *chatti*. Two miles further on we found an oasis in the desert. The bare mountainside had been transformed by springs of water into a cool shady garden and we were able to buy fresh onions and potatoes, a great luxury.

Studying my map I imagined that if I could climb out of the valley and get to the top of a nearby peak I could probably see Nanda Devi, 25,600 feet, the highest mountain in the British Empire. All the side valleys seemed to point in the wrong direction, and between us and Nanda Devi towered the Trisul range with its 23,000 feet peaks. Enquiries along the route produced no-one who had any idea what could be seen over the ridge.

We arrived at Garurganga, a small tributary of the Ganges, which here dashes down the mountainside to join the Alaknanda 2,000 feet below the road. It is named after the fabulous bird which is the vehicle of the god Vishnu. There is an important temple here, with a pool where the pilgrims bathe. It was a lovely clear evening and we looked round for somewhere to sleep in the open and we found an almost flat place beside a stream that had been diverted so as to turn the wheels of several little cornmills.

Next day's march brought us to another tributary and another temple, Patalganga, named after the Ganges of the Infernal Region. The name may have been suggested by the extraordinary nature of the valley. The track passes near the bottom of an almost perpendicular cliff of great height, with an exceedingly steep mountainside immediately opposite. Sometimes big rocks get dislodged and come hurtling down destroying part of the roadway. By the village the two sides are so close that the tributary is spanned by a short wooden bridge.

Enquiring here I began to hear rumours of a man who roamed the mountains and might be a reliable guide. That afternoon we unexpectedly encountered the very man. Dressed in a thick grey wool homespun coat and trousers, which hillmen wear till they drop off, Ajab Singh said he knew Nanda Devi, and agreed after some haggling to take us to where we could see the peak.

Early next morning we were soon rising by sharp zig-zags above the village. We passed through a belt of terraced golden wheat fields, on steep hillside pastures and into a thick forest of rhododendron and oak. It was a stiff climb and the soles of our sandals had become polished by the dry leaves on the ground. Progress slowed and the constant slipping was exhausting. At last we emerged from the forest onto a broad mountain pasture, wet with dew, and the slope less steep.

Ajab Singh was an interesting talker, a veritable mine of information. He pointed out medicinal plants, the quality of wood of the different trees and bushes, and promised to present us each with a stick for our travels so that we might never forget him. He asked if we were married and what family we had. He told us of his disappointment at not having children though he had four wives all living, and asked if we thought he should take a fifth. Like Job his wealth was his flocks and herds and we saw some of his

Ajab Singh, our guide.

beautiful goats with their long white silky hair, and his magnificent hill dogs with their thick coats and spiked collars to protect them from panthers.

By nine o'clock we had climbed 3,000 feet in about three miles. We sat down and ate a dry chapati each by a pure mountain spring. Ajab Singh produced a few walnuts from his pocket. Starting again Ajab remarked, 'In a few minutes you will see Nanda Devi and you will have to give me Rs.5 *bakshish* for having shown you the sacred mountain'. Presently we rounded a shoulder from which several peaks were visible and Ajab Singh pointed to one in the distance saying, 'There is Nanda Devi; now the object of our climb is attained'. I was not convinced. From what I had seen near Tungnath I felt Nanda Devi was still hidden by the summit of Oli Gursal, the 12,500 feet mountain on which we stood. The summit appeared about a mile further on and I suggested we should proceed. Ajab Singh maintained he had kept his side of the bargain and did not intend to go any further. He went on to say that it was impossible to reach the summit as there were precipices in the way, and the forest was infested with bears and panthers. So I set off on my own telling Khushilal and Ajab Singh to await my return.

I soon found a little track through the forest – no wild animals barred my way, and I again emerged in the open where blue and purple iris, and anemones abounded. I hurried on hoping to reach the summit in about half an hour, not realising it was another three miles and 3,000 feet above me, the clear air being so deceptive. The summit got no nearer, and my sandals more slippery. At last I had to take them off and go barefoot over the rough vegetation and through the patches of snow. The altitude and exertion made breathing difficult and I had to rest to allow my thumping heart to quieten down. Almost exactly at noon I staggered up the final rocky point and stood on the summit. The view was worth it all. I was surrounded by a circle of snowy peaks, though by that time Nanda Devi and several others were partially obscured by clouds. Nearby was the first peak of the great Trisul range, which for 20 miles does not drop below 20,000 feet. I hastily took a few photographs and barely recovered my breath before starting down again. Slipping and sliding and running wherever possible, I managed the return journey in under two hours, having been away nearly five hours.

I found the others in a great state having given me up for dead; preparing to organise a search party. Ajab Singh was sure his reputation as a guide had been lost for ever, and Khushilal had been wondering how he would ever face my wife and friends again.

On the way down Ajab Singh kept his promise to cut us sticks. He lit a fire for heating and straightening the sticks, while some of his flocks, with one of his wives in charge, passed along the hillside 1,000 feet above us. As is the custom in the hills, they kept up a conversation as long as they could see each other.

The descent was more slippery than the ascent, and several times I lost my footing and fell heavily. Back on the pilgrim road I had had enough climbing to last me for a long time to come. Ajab

The Trisul Ridge, from the summit of Oli Gursal (foreground).

Singh had been provided with a topic of conversation he will not forget for quite a while.

Joshimath to Badrinath

The next day's march brought us to Joshimath. Joshimath is important as it is the headquarters of the Rawal (High Priest) of Badrinath during the long months when Badrinath is under snow. There are several temples here, a bazaar, post office and police station. We bought some milk at the exorbitant price of 12 *annas* a *seer*, but it tasted more like Epsom salts than milk, and I gave it to a huge sheepdog that had been watching me hungrily.

Leaving Joshimath the road zig-zags down the mountain for two miles to the junction with the Alaknanda (from this point called the Vishnuganga) and the Dhauli river. The road to Badrinath and beyond to the Mana Pass and Tibet follows the Vishnuganga, and the road to Tibet via the Niti Pass, leading to Mansarower Lake and Kailasa Mountain, follows the Dhauli river.

No European is supposed to go beyond Vishnuprayag without special permission from the Deputy Commissioner of Garhwal. This restriction was to prevent Europeans reaching Tibet. I had not heard of the restriction, so went across the 'Inner Line' and up to Badrinath without permission.

The bathing at Vishnuprayag is most dangerous as both rivers are extremely swift. Chains to hang onto are arranged to protect bathers from the current, but many people are carried away and drowned each year. Some of the finest scenery is met in this area. The gorge is narrow and the sides precipitous. The *chhir* pines cling to the face of the mountain, and further up give way to other conifers and horse chestnuts. Amongst them we found a number of *deodar* trees, the Himalayan cedar, which are scarce along the pilgrim route.

In this final stage of the journey is a village called Pandukeshwar, where there are two temples side by side. This is the traditional birthplace of the five Pandava brothers. We passed straight through the village as we were anxious to reach Lambagar, ready to make a final sprint for Badrinath in the morning.

After a cold night we were glad to be on the move by 5 a.m. As far as Hanuman *chatti*, three miles on, the road is not difficult and the scenery lovely. Masses of white wild roses and clematis scent the air. Legend has it that in ancient times King Marut offered a great sacrifice at the hermitage of a sage. All the ceremony vessels were of gold, and all the gods gathered for the sacrifice. It is said the mountain was formed by the ashes left after the sacrifice. This can be tested by any pilgrim if he digs near the peak, where he will be certain to find scorched grains of barley and sesame seeds.

Above Hanuman *chatti* all trees are left behind. The remaining four miles to Badrinath are a severe test of physical fitness. The path too is dangerous, offering very insecure foothold where it had been undermined or worn away by trickling water. Several times we crossed places where there had been small avalanches, and where the snow had not melted, there was a danger of sliding down the slope into the river some distance below.

At the steepest part of the road we overtook a thin, old woman. We could not understand what she wanted. Then she snatched hold of Khushilal's stick, and we understood. Khushilal's stick was a heavy one, so I gave her mine instead and she was very thankful. Several days later we overtook her again. I recognised the stick before the woman and hoped she might give me back my stick as it was the one Ajab Singh had given me. But she did not want to part with it and I expect she has it yet.

Two miles from Badrinath we began meeting a stream of pilgrims coming down. Many of them seemed in great spirits and met us poor breathless people with shouts of '*Bolo, Badri Bishal kijay*' (Shout, victory to Badrinath). One *sadhu* who had seen me before, coming down the hill at about six miles an hour, called out to me in English, 'Chant "OM" my dear Sir, chant "OM"' – but I had no spare breath for chanting the mystical syllable, even if I had believed in its efficacy.

Badrinath

The seemingly endless climb came to an end and we reached the ridge from which, a mile ahead, the temple and village of Badrinath can be seen. This is known as Deodekhni – vision of God. Pilgrims catching their first sight of the temple prostrate themselves and touch the ground with their foreheads. Some remove their shoes and walk barefoot from here.

To reach the town the river has to be crossed once more by a wooden bridge. Before crossing the bridge we called at the Government hospital in the hope the doctor could find us somewhere to lodge rather than face the bazaar conditions. He very kindly arranged for us to use a small room in a new *dharmshala*, not yet open to the public, and we were very thankful to be so well off. When the doctor heard I was not feeling very well he sent food from his own house. It was not his first season at Badrinath, so he knew a good deal about the residents and the pilgrims, and told us that many of the latter were torn between the desire to recover and the desire to die in such a holy place, and so be assured of deliverance from the results of their sins. They would come to him for advice, but could not accept his treatment. Sometimes he had to turn them away, explaining that if they must die, the hospital compound was not the place to commit suicide.

On the evening of our arrival I went to see the temple. I did not go in, but looking down from above could see the preparation of the *bhog* – 'the food offered to idols'. This is prepared by people of a special hereditary caste. They are paid by temple funds and have the right to sell the food after it has been offered. The temple is sacred to Vishnu, and the architecture is like that seen on the plains of North India, and unlike the Kedarnath style seen everywhere else. It is said to owe its foundation to Shankaracharya, who lived in the 8th century AD. The building has been repeatedly devastated by earthquakes and avalanches, and has no appearance of great antiquity. There is a tradition that the idol was thrown into the Alaknanda by Buddhists, and was miraculously recovered by Shankaracharya. Below the temple is a warm sulphur spring. Here pilgrims settle their accounts with their *pandas*, who when satisfied that they have got all they can out of them, give the pilgrims their assurance of the success of the pilgrimage.

The first night was very cold, but I slept in all the clothes I had with me and did not suffer. Khushilal and the *coolies* found it trying, so we decided we would have to leave that afternoon. Like the majority of pilgrims we could not afford dry wood for cooking, which was brought up the hill early in the morning, and quickly bought up by residents in the know. Wet wood was unsuitable for cooking or warmth but was all that was available for the poorer pilgrims. Some of the town's people asked me to explain their difficulties to the Deputy Commissioner, and this I was able to do later and give witness from my own experience of the hardship caused to the pilgrims.

We had decided to leave when a most interesting visitor was announced. He was a *sadhu* named Ram Sarikh Singh who had lived in Badrinath for the last three hot seasons. Somehow he had heard of our difficulties and sent a bundle of firewood and a generous supply of food, including a *seer* of milk. Later he turned up with blankets which we had to refuse as the doctor had already supplied us with hospital blankets; so we changed our minds and gratefully stayed on.

Swami Ram Sarikh Singh stayed and took *chotti haziri* with us – tea made with the milk he had provided and boiled on the wood he had sent. Then he took us on a guided excursion to Mana village where the Marchhas live – people with Tibetan features and rosy cheeks. They can only live here for six months as the rest of the year it is under snow. Mana is at the northern end of the oval valley that Badrinath is at the southern, and is the last village before the border. The road goes on for another 40 miles till it crosses the 17,000 feet Mana Pass leading to Tibet. The Marchhas are Hindus. As Badrinath is within their territory they receive annual payment from the temple and the women lead the procession on the day of the Janam Ashtami festival when the god is taken from the temple to a place nearby called Mata Murati, where the idol is bathed at the waterfall and fed.

On both sides of the valley are high mountains. Our objective was the river Sarsuti, which joins the Alaknanda at the northern end of the valley. After flowing for two miles under a huge land-slide, it enters the valley out of what appears at first sight to be a solid cliff, and comes leaping down a succession of small falls, overflowing from one cauldron to another. At one place it is spanned by an enormous block of stone forming a natural bridge. A flock of sheep crossing this rock in single file look no bigger than currants on a rock bun. The water is crystal clear, light blue – a striking contrast to the opaque grey water of the Alaknanda, in which it is soon to be merged.

High up on the cliff above is a cave known as Vyas Gufa, which was the hermitage of the sage Vyas Muni, and where he compiled the Puran and the Mahabharata.

The natural bridge over the Sarsuti river at Mana village. Sheep crossing it are just discernible, centre right.

We had accepted an invitation to breakfast provided by the Kalikamliwalas, and had promised to be back by 11 o'clock. Where most people tell the time by the sun, a certain amount of latitude is allowed in keeping appointments. In spite of my intention to return in good time, I suffer the Englishman's craze to see just round the next corner. Having seen the natural bridge, the view further up the Alaknanda looked so tempting, we decided to go just a little further. After an exhausting climb we reached a little knoll, from which the glacier, which is the main source of the Alaknanda, was visible. Just to the left of that, hidden behind the shoulder of a hill, is the famous Satopanth glacier, and I now regret that I did not go on and see what was around the next corner for I would have been able to see right up the Satopanth glacier to the mighty peaks of Chaukhamba. As it was, straight in front of us was the magnificent Kunaling Peak, nearly 23,000 feet. To the right of it was the Bhagat Kharak glacier, and where the two glaciers met was what I thought was the source of the Alaknanda.

Turning round from where I stood I could also see the 700 feet Basudhara waterfall, reckoned by some pilgrims as one of the most important sights of the pilgrimage, but on this occasion there was so little water I was unimpressed.

It was 1.30 p.m. before we returned tired out to claim our breakfast. We had covered eight miles of hard going in seven hours, sustained only by two cups of tea before we started.

Kunaling Peak, with Chaukhamba behind, and the Bhagat glacier, meeting the Satopanth glacier at its foot, with the black spot I thought must be the source of the Alaknanda in 1923 (see p. 89).

Later that evening I went a little way up the Rishiganga valley at the head of which stands Nalikanta, 21,713 feet – a perfect symmetrical peak, five miles away, but looking much closer in the clear air. Bathed in moonlight it rose majestic from the lower hills and valley still in darkness.

The Return Journey

The time came to tear ourselves away from Badrinath. Swami Ram Sarikh Singh accompanied us the two miles downhill and it was hard to leave him. At this early hour there was a steady stream of Marchha women carrying heavy loads of wood up the mountainside that had so tested our powers only two days before when we were carrying nothing. It was much easier going downhill and we swung along at a good pace.

We stopped for our midday meal at Lambagar. A *sadhu* in great distress told me he had been robbed of a Rs.100 note, and so was now destitute. He suspected his *coolie*, as only he could have known that the note was tucked in his waist cloth. Considering the conditions of the pilgrimage, it is surprising there is not more crime.

I did not hear of more than two or three cases of theft, one of which had proved to be a false alarm.

Late afternoon found us back at Vishnuprayag, 17 miles from Badrinath, where it was much warmer and we were quite comfortable sleeping out on a level piece of ground near the suspension bridge, lulled to sleep by the roar of the Dhauli river. By 3.15 a.m. a long procession of sheep and goats poured across the bridge, issuing one by one three feet from our heads. The pattering of their feet seemed endless and then there was quiet again. Not for long – soon the early pilgrims were on the move. By 5 a.m. we ourselves were off to tackle the long climb by the short cut, avoiding Joshimath, before the heat of the sun fell on our backs.

By the afternoon of the third day we were back in Chamoli and I went to the government hospital to have my little toe dressed. I had been walking for the past week with a blister which had been gradually getting worse. The treatment did it good, but the constant walking meant it never got a chance to heal all the way back to Hardwar, which meant I had endured it for over 200 miles.

I had heard that the Indian magistrate at Chamoli, the *Tahsildar*, was a friendly sort of person, and that his father had been a great authority on Garhwal, and had written a book about it. So I called on him and he spent some time telling me the history of the district, and when leaving kindly presented me with a copy of his father's book which is now difficult to obtain. Khushilal and the *coolies* had gone on ahead, and I set off alone on the four miles to where we had agreed to spend the night. I fell in with a *sadhu* going the same way. He was dressed only in a loin cloth and a fur hat. He was a man of wide experience and considerable interest. Before long he noticed I was finding my load very heavy, made so by the accumulation of mail I had picked up at Chamoli, and insisted on taking it out of sheer kindness. He refused the offer of a meal on our arrival, and I suspect went without food that night. Next morning we saluted him when we started before him, but we never saw him again.

We had done 50 miles in three days determined to get home as quickly as possible, as we were both feeling the physical and mental strain. But after the midday halt next day I noticed Khushilal was not well. He had severe internal pain and with difficulty dragged himself to the next *chatti* a mile further on. The *chatti* was pleasantly situated where the valley widened, and there was flat ground nearby to spread out our bedding. We were seven miles from the nearest hospital and still 100 miles or more from the railway, so I had no alternative but to try the treatment described in the fifth chapter of the Epistle of James. All around us pilgrims were cooking their evening meal. We lay down and waited till darkness fell. Khushilal became worse; by now he had a high fever and was delirious, saying all sorts of ridiculous things. As the noise died down, I bent over him, laid my hands on him, and prayed that he might be healed in the name of Jesus Christ. While I was still bending over him he sat up and began talking normally. Gopal Singh came over to see what had happened. The fever and pain had gone, and we were able to do an ordinary march next day. Gopal Singh kept asking Khushilal to explain what had happened, and the day we parted from him at Rishikesh, he said to Khushilal, 'One thing I have learned in living with you two all this time is that if anyone is ill, he should pray in the name of Jesus Christ'.

Karnprayag is the last of the five great sacred bathing junctions, where the Pindar river joins the Alaknanda, and here the road divides and the main stream of pilgrims turn south and make for the railway at Ramnagar. I called at the Post Office, but there were no letters. The clerk told me that the Deputy Commissioner was expected that day and invited me to spend the time with him so that I could have an interview. I decided to take the opportunity to plead the cause of the pilgrims, and explain the hardship suffered due to the lack of dry wood for cooking at Badrinath.

Khushilal and the *coolies* had gone on ahead expecting me to follow immediately. Khushilal looked after our money, so I only had six *annas* on me. By 5 p.m. I was extremely hungry and went for a walk, returning at 7 p.m. to find that the postmaster had intercepted two letters – one returning down after missing me, and another on its way up, so I felt justified in staying. The Deputy Commissioner arrived about 8 p.m. accompanied by an army officer who had been hunting. They welcomed me warmly and plied me with questions, and then offered me dinner. I refused as I thought my friend had already started to cook for me. I returned at 9.30 expecting a meal to be ready, but to my horror my friend had not fully trusted my promise to return, and had waited to see whether I had changed my mind. So it was after 10 p.m. before my hunger was assuaged. At 11 p.m. a note came from the Deputy Commissioner inviting me to stay as long as I liked with him at Pauri, the district headquarters, three days' march away.

We arrived the day before the Deputy Commissioner was expected home, so went to the American Methodist Mission in Pauri, where we were welcomed by Rev and Mrs Weak. The Mission High School was the only High School in Garhwal. A new larger High School was under construction to accommodate 500 boys. Pauri is at an altitude of 5,000 feet so every stone and all the timber has to be brought up on the backs of *coolies* from the Ganges, eight miles away and 4,000 feet below – so it's no mean feat. In spite of almost superhuman difficulties the work is nearing completion. The site is on the side of the mountain, and the buildings stand on terraces cut out one above the other. A good-sized playing field has been cut out for the boys to play their favourite game, football, but a lot of time seemed to be spent on recovering the ball from great distances below!

The following day I moved into the Deputy Commissioner's guest bungalow, a delightful spot in woods 1,000 feet higher up the mountain. Due to the hot weather haze, the line of snowy peaks, including Kedarnath and Badrinath, was not visible. Here I had six days of real holiday, Mr and Mrs Acton making me just one of the family. I wondered what the Mohammedan butler thought of me when he waited at meal-times on a barefoot English pilgrim. It was not easy to tear myself away and take to the road again.

The day we left Pauri we attempted a double march. We had parted with the second *coolie* and were carrying our own loads again. The first 10 miles along level ground were easy, but after the midday halt we had to take a little-used side road, which in nine miles was to bring us back to the Ganges 4,000 feet below. All afternoon we seemed to be dodging thunderstorms, the road was rough and our loads heavy. Beside which I was suffering from six days of over-indulging in the hospitality of my friends in Pauri. At 4.15 p.m. we came to the saddle of a ridge, on which there stood a magnificent tree, round the foot of which was built a raised platform, or *charbutra*, and a shrine in honour of the spirit that was supposed to dwell there. From the ridge there was a fine view right down a straight stretch of the Ganges valley, where we could see, more than four miles away and a long way down, the silver streak of the river, shining in the afternoon sun. The road was so bad, and the continual descent so tiring, that even Gopal Singh was tired out. It took us three hours to do the distance, and it was nearly dark when we arrived dead beat. Gopal Singh just lay down and refused to move until Khushilal insisted that he get something to eat. Khushilal felt as bad, but for my sake heated some milk and we shared some bread Mrs Acton had given me for the journey. Then we all lay down and never stirred till morning.

Two days later we were within four miles of Lachhman Jhula and back to civilisation and our last night on the road. There had been a heavy thunderstorm in the afternoon. I left Khushilal cooking on the sand in front of the *chatti* and went off for a bathe in the Hiul river just above the junction. I was happily soaking in a nice pool when some fishermen came along unexpectedly. They threw a huge net over the pool and I only just escaped being caught. They rushed into the water to secure their catch and discovered me. At first I thought they were going to make a dash at me, but I succeeded in making them understand I was harmless, and they quickly gathered up their net and made off. When I returned the cooking was nearing completion, but a sudden gust of wind sent sparks of wood from Khushilal's fire 50 yards along the sand. We rescued what we could, but most of the food was scattered over the sand and uneatable. When we were settling down for the night, Khushilal noticed a scorpion walk out of his bedding. A search was organised but it disappeared, so we were uneasy – these mountain scorpions are unpleasant bedfellows. The rain brought out a plague of squashy-bodied insects. I spent most of the night catching them and throwing them outside. It was a relief when day broke.

Before reaching Lachhman Jhula we came to the flourishing banana garden where on the way up the caretaker had refused to sell me any bananas. There was nothing left but gaunt stems; the whole area had been devastated by a plague of locusts.

Back in Rishikesh we packed our things in a *tonga* ready for departure. We were sorry to leave Gopal Singh and he was obviously sad at our going. He watched us till we were nearly out of sight before finally turning away.

That afternoon we arrived in Hardwar and I outwardly became an Englishman again. My last vision of the pilgrimage was a crowd of fresh pilgrims pouring through the station gate and being confronted outside by the many *pandas* lying in wait for them.

PART III
PRELIMINARY: THE AMARNATH
PILGRIMAGE 1929

THE AMARNATH PILGRIMAGE IN 1929 was led by Swami Shiv Ratan Gir and from the Hindu point of view was a great success. Swami Shiv Ratan Gir had done the pilgrimage 35 times and said he had never known the weather to be so favourable. The previous year, 1928, had been disastrous. There had been 136 hours of continuous rain and many pilgrims lost their lives. In one respect they did not die in vain as the Kashmir authorities have spared no efforts to make the pilgrimage as safe as humanly possible. Large sums of money have been spent on repairing and widening the road, and in some places making a new road altogether. Nowhere was it necessary to wade through streams of ice-cold water, as bridges had been constructed and stones placed across the smaller streams. At the recognised halting places, sheds with iron roofs had been built, which, though not yet sufficient for the need, go a long way towards it.

Provision of meal tickets for needy *sadhus*, firewood for cooking, *coolies* to help with loads and ponies for the infirm, had already been thought of and supplied. Together with the Revenue Minister, a large contingent of police, a medical team of four doctors with a staff of compounders and dressers, I had been invited to accompany the 1929 pilgrimage, to see if I could make any further suggestions for the well-being of the pilgrims and *coolies*.

Motor lorries have shortened the pilgrimage for most pilgrims, and the real pilgrimage now starts at Pahalgam. As we started out a census was taken:

	Men	Women	Children	Total
Sadhus	689	22	2	713
Punjabis	434	232	72	738
Kashmiri Pandits	552	132	11	695
				2146

Along with these pilgrims went a small army of 1,055 *coolies* and 1,018 ponies. Of the ponies, 378 were for riding and 640 for luggage.

57

The first stage from Pahalgam to Chhandanwari is an easy one, following the Lidar river through beautiful forest scenery, but the next stage is more strenuous. A formidable pass, Pissu Ghati, a climb of 1,500 feet, has to be faced. Two or three miles of easier walking brings the pilgrims to Zajpal Pass, after ascending which the beautiful little Lake Sheshnag is reached at 12,000 feet. Many pilgrims bathe here, though it is too cold to stay in for more than a few seconds. A mile further on the main camp at Wavajan is reached.

Leaving Wavajan the next morning the Mahagunas Pass, 14,500 feet, is crossed. It was up here we saw several skeletons bearing witness to the terrible nature of the disaster the previous year. The approach to the Mahagunas Pass from either direction is an easier gradient than the other passes, but the altitude taxes the strength of most pilgrims.

Six miles follow of comparatively easy going to Panchtarni, where five glacier-fed streams unite to form a tributary of the Sind river.

Panchtarni is the last camp. Even before midnight the stream of pilgrims begins to leave for the Amarnath cave. All through the night the procession goes on. In the light of the full moon the zig-zag road can be traced up the mountainside by the twinkling lights of the lanterns they carry. They disappear over a shoulder into the valley of the Amarwali stream, at the head of which the cave can be seen some distance up the mountain.

The bottom of the valley is full of snow, but this year there is much less than usual. By 6 a.m. there were hundreds of pilgrims assembled, some bathing in the stream beside the cave, others going up and down from worshipping in the cave. At the back of the cave are the three blocks of ice representing Shiv, Parbuti and Ganesh, on which water drops from the roof and freezes. Pilgrims crowd round making their offerings of cloth, flowers, rice and coconuts, so the ice was almost covered over. Some tried to catch drops of water in their mouths, while others collected it in bottles. Every now and again the shout would go up, '*Bolo, Amarnath Swami ki jai*', and all would join in.

As soon as the *darshan* is completed the pilgrims hurry back to Panchtarni and the more energetic ones can actually reach Pahalgam the same day. The old short-cut by Astanmarg is now considered too dangerous. More venturesome *sadhus* who care little if they lose their lives in this sacred place prefer this road, which leads past Hatyara Talab, a picturesque lake with a background of snowy peaks, which gets its name from a tradition that once hundreds of pilgrims lost their lives there in a heavy fall of snow.

By late afternoon the Amarnath cave is left deserted and silent, and the pigeons return to their quiet abode.

PART III
THE 1930 PILGRIMAGE

CHAPTER 5

The Road Again

Give me my scallop-shell of quiet,
My staff of faith to walk upon,
My scrip of joy, immortal diet,
My bottle of salvation,
My gown of glory, hope's true gage;
And thus I'll take my pilgrimage.
(Sir Walter Raleigh)

WHEN I RETURNED HOME from Badrinath in 1923, I was sure that I had been within sight of the source of the Alaknanda, and that when I examined the photograph of Kunaling peak, I would be able to identify where the river bursts forth from the Satopanth glacier. But when I compared the photograph with the map, I reluctantly had to admit that I could not possibly have seen the true source. So it was inevitable from then on that I would have to return.

I managed to convince myself that a second journey might even be more fruitful, and I must admit that the pilgrimage had a continuing fascination for me, urging me to undertake further adventures on the same lines and fill other gaps in my photographic record, notably a view of the Kedarnath temple on which I had set my heart.

Though my personal inclination was in favour of going again, I had to satisfy myself that it was right for me to go. The first pilgrimage had been undertaken under a strong feeling of concern – to use the Quaker term – and I was convinced it was right to go. That being so, whatever difficulties and dangers we encountered, there was no need to be anxious. But now other considerations had arisen, and my motives were to some extent mixed. Although my wife always loyally promised she would never stand in my way, she knew enough of the conditions and risks of the road to make her anxious. As I could only undertake these journeys in the hot weather when she and the children were in England, it was debatable whether I was acting fairly towards my family. I also had to ask myself whether I was justified in asking Khushilal to undergo the same hardships, as he was also married and had a larger family than my own.

However it was seven years before the opportunity occurred and by that time, I felt it was right for me to go. Khushilal was equally keen. From our first experience, I was convinced that wearing the ochre-coloured *sadhu* dress had been more of a help than a hindrance. The previous year I had been on the Amarnarth pilgrimage in Kashmir and brought back two Kashmiri *kiltas*, wicker baskets, covered in thin leather, with lids that could be padlocked, thinking they would be as good as the *kandi* type baskets used by the *coolies*. In practice they were not a success. I had also given much thought and time to planning other improvements in our equipment and the route, and remembered to obtain a permit from the Deputy Commissioner at Pauri to cross the 'inner frontier' and also a permit to use PWD bungalows in case of need. Once we had these we were ready to set off.

After 27 hours in the stifling atmosphere of packed third class compartments, we arrived at Hardwar on the afternoon of 1 May 1930. The usual crowd of *pandas* was waiting for the pilgrims as they poured out of the gateway. They looked at us, but we passed through them with the comfortable feeling of knowing what we were doing, and made our way to the Dak bungalow, to be greeted by the same friendly Mohammedan *khansama*, as glad to see us as we were to see him.

The postmaster also remembered us when we went to make arrangements for forwarding our letters, before walking on to the sacred bathing-pool, Har ki Pairi, in the cool of the evening. In other parts of India there was unrest owing to the Non-cooperation Movement, and we fancied there was less friendliness than before, and wondered how we would be received by the pilgrims on the road.

We were up early next morning. Khushilal put the finishing touches to my *turban*, and we were ready for the road. We took a *tonga* to the motor stand, where a *coolie* spotted us and was so anxious that we engage him that he hurried on ahead to Rishikesh, the recognised place for engaging *coolies*. Though it was risky I took a liking to the man and we had no reason to regret our choice. There were plenty of *coolies* waiting around, and we asked the agent who recognised us to chose another for us. He turned out to be lazy and left all the extra jobs to the man we had chosen first.

The price of wheat in Tehri State had fallen, so the rate of payment was Rs.65. for each *coolie*, Rs.10 less than seven years ago.

By the time all the arrangements had been concluded we were quite ready for a meal. We found a shady place under an ancient *peepul* tree, not far from our first camping place in 1923, close by the water's edge. I squatted on the ground with a pile of *puris* and some potato curry in a leaf bowl. A baby monkey came and sat opposite, making pathetic wailing noises. While I was watching him, and as I raised my hand to my mouth, a huge monkey darted round the trunk of the tree, helped himself to two *puris* and made off. I had to protect the rest of my meal with my hill stick in one hand while I ate with the other.

The old suspension bridge at Lachhman Jhula, which we had crossed in 1923, had been washed away in a flood in 1924. Fortunately for us the Governor of the United Provinces had only three weeks before opened a new bridge. This one was longer and 59 feet above the summer level of the river. The Ganges, unlike the rivers of the plains, has its highest levels in the summer when the snow melts.

In a few minutes a bend in the river hid the great suspension bridge and the temples on either side. We had set our feet again on the pilgrim road, this time not as complete strangers, but with confidence, because we knew what to expect. The worries and burdens of daily life had been left behind, we were stepping out into new adventures, going to make new friends and renew old acquaintances.

We went further than intended that first night, as the *coolies* did not favour my choice of *chatti*, so we were later in settling than I should have liked. A great deal depends on the acquaintances made in the first few days, as they are people we meet day after day at the midday halt and in the evenings. The more friends you make the less of a stranger you feel when the *chattis* are crowded and accommodation scarce. The fact that we knew the road and could give reliable information was an asset, and many pilgrims showed us great respect for the merit we had surely gained by completing the pilgrimage once already.

So it was with special interest that I surveyed my fellow travellers. Most were too busy with their own affairs, but while Khushilal was cooking, I discovered a party of *sannyasis*, dressed in the same style as we were. There were eight of them. I approached them and conversation began in Hindi, until an older *sannyasi* joined us, and addressed me in English whereupon I took the line of least resistance and replied in my mother tongue. This man was obviously highly respected by the rest of the group. He asked me about my clothes and spoke of the necessity of renunciation as well as the outward appearance. 'A true *sannyasi* is a seeker, but so few people honestly devote themselves to seeking.' This gave me the opportunity to describe our method of worship. He had heard of Quakers, but was under the impression that they quaked or danced. He told me of the Vaishnava sect that met in silence and waited for inspiration. I soon discovered that this man had a degree from the Scottish Churches College, Calcutta, and was well acquainted with the Bible, which he quoted fluently.

Later I was to learn that this *sannyasi*, Swami Bisshuddhanand, had been headmaster of a government Secondary School. He had somehow been implicated in what was known as the 'Alipur Bomb Case', and had subsequently served a term of penal servitude in the Andaman Islands. Our friendship has continued on and off till the present time and I find it hard to believe he could harm any living creature. Eight years later, when I was visiting him in the headquarters of his sect in Hardwar, plain-clothes detectives made a remark which told me that his record is still remembered.

Khushilal called me for supper and I excused myself remarking that I hoped we would see each other on the road in the morning. The night was hot and after the excitements of the first day I could not sleep. At last I slept but the racket of pilgrims preparing to start woke me at 4.10 a.m. By 5 o'clock I was packed and the *coolies* were off ahead with their loads. I went down to the river to find a private place to wash. I have never succeeded in overcoming the Englishman's preference for washing, shaving and bathing in privacy, and often wish for a brown skin, so as not to be so conspicuous. I regret that on occasions I have gone dirty rather than perform my ablutions along with the other pilgrims. On this occasion I found a small pool at the foot of an overhanging rock, and had a swim, returning refreshed to the *chatti* after most of the pilgrims had left. The *sannyasi* party was still in their *chatti*, and I was told the leader was suffering from dysentery and unable to travel. The leader was under a vow of silence, and for that reason was always referred to as 'Moni Maharaj'. He kept his vow through the whole journey, communicating his wishes by signs, and in a last resort by writing instructions. Swami B. (as I shall henceforth refer to him) by seniority and character should have been the leader, and often bemoaned his fate.

I did have dysentery tablets in my luggage, which had gone on ahead with the *coolies*, so I promised to look for them if they caught us up. As he could not say when they would be following, it was uncertain whether we would meet again, so I lingered awhile. He told me he had not been a *sadhu* since boyhood, as was the custom now, but had followed the ancient Hindu rule of life and had entered the 'fourth stage', that of renunciation, after he reached the age of 50. As we parted he said, 'You will understand the meaning of my name, "Perfect Bliss", but though I am seeking that bliss, I have not yet found it, but I hope to do so.'

Before long I overtook an old pilgrim with white hair and beard, quietly repeating the word 'Ram' every six steps. Occasionally he varied it by chanting 'Ram, Ram, Sita Ram'. He caught me up at the top of a long climb over the ridge. The fable of the hare and the tortoise is frequently illustrated on the pilgrimage. He was still repeating the name. Several days later we caught up with him again, still breathing the name of 'Ram' every sixth step. His rope-soled shoes were already worn out, but he still went ahead like a machine. He told me he was a *kachhi* (market gardener) by caste, and had taken up the wandering life three years ago. He intended spending the rest of his life travelling from one sacred place to another.

On the long steep descent back to the Ganges that had proved such a severe test to our knees in 1923, I developed a blister on my heel. When I stopped the *coolies* to get out another pair of shoes, I found I had lost my keys. However it did not take much to bend the chain and slip the padlock through.

Instead of going to a crowded *chatti* we stopped at midday by a little spring where there was some shade. There were not many pilgrims behind us, but I heard someone calling from the zig-zag path above us. A blind man had dropped his stick and it had gone over the edge. I climbed up and rescued it. The old man's companion was so grateful, he repaid me by gathering wood for our fire.

I had given in to weakness and provided myself with some extras for the road. These luxuries were a supply of tea, a 2 lb. tin of Klim dried milk powder, and a string of dried figs – included for their medicinal property. I planned to eat two or three of them every morning as long as they lasted. They were hard and dry and took 20 minutes to chew to get the maximum taste out of them, so I had to shun the society of my fellow pilgrims until I had disposed of them. Later this habit complicated my relationship with the *sannyasi* party, as did the tea, as I could not indulge in tea drinking by myself, and there was insufficient to supply them all. So sometimes I had to go without when I was dying for a cup of tea. The *sannyasis* quenched their thirst with unboiled water – a risk I could not take – and it was quicker to have a drink of tea than wait while the boiled water cooled down.

I tried when possible not to march on a Sunday, and plan to stop at a PWD engineer's bungalow. It's an opportunity to catch up with letter writing, reading and meditating, with the added comfort of a bed, table and chair. The *coolies* never like resting on a Sunday, even though they are paid to do nothing, and were always anxious and impatient to be off. On this occasion the bungalow was hot and uninviting, and threatening clouds had gathered, so we decided to set off for an afternoon march. I was waiting for Khushilal to have a drink at a 'Pya-u' when I noticed a sunbird flitting about in some bushes, and suddenly disappear into what looked like a little bundle of rubbish. The apparent rubbish was its nest – a very clever piece of work, with a circular door and overhanging porch. I have seen three such nests, all close to the path, and only noticed when the bird itself gives the secret away.

By encouraging the *coolies* to put a spurt on, we managed to reach shelter before the downpour began. We selected a nice quiet corner in an upper room, and after the rain was over I went out to see if I could find some old friends. Several *chatti*-keepers remembered us passing through last time. I went to the small government hospital, as it is always useful to make friends with the doctor, and being isolated they appreciate any sign of friendship. The doctor was a Garhwali, an old student of the American Methodist High School. I learnt from him that he had had a patient with cholera, and I made a mental note to remember to be extra careful to boil the drinking water. Another case was a man who had dislocated and fractured his hip by falling over a wall in the dark when he needed a private place to relieve himself. He had been brought to hospital in a *dandi*, and in spite of being in great pain refused to stop. A sick woman I had advised to go to the hospital had not done so. The doctor explained that patients often will not go to see the doctor as they are afraid of being hindered on their journey or otherwise prevented from going on. The *coolies* also discourage them, as they would lose their job if they were detained, and often tell them the hospital is further on.

On our return to the *chatti* a party of Punjabis, mostly women, had joined us in our upper room. The women chattered like jackdaws and were very noisy in settling down. And that reminds me that just on a level with the corner where I sat, looking through the open side of the room, there was a magpie sitting on her nest.

During the following afternoon I noticed an inscription on the face of a big smooth rock, 'Khadar pahirna dharm hai videshi pahirna pap hai', (It is a religious duty to wear Indian cloth, it is a sin to wear foreign cloth). Politics seemed so far from the mind of the average pilgrim that I had almost begun to forget non-cooperation, and all its excitements. We were in a hurry as I wanted to catch the post at Devaprayag, one of the few reliable post offices. It had moved from the pilgrim roadside to the centre of the bazaar, and the postmaster who had given me 'a place for the sole of my foot' last time had been transferred. But I found a Mohammedan (very scarce in these parts) and a *chama* (leather worker) who remembered me, and were pleased to be remembered.

At Devaprayag I yielded to temptation and occupied the PWD bungalow. These bungalows usually enjoy a good position and this one was no exception, high on the hillside overlooking the town and the river. It was quiet and peaceful, clean and comparatively free from flies.

A roadside post office at Agastyamuni,
between Rudraprayag and Guptkashi.

The following morning after a drink of tea and masticating three dried figs, I set off with Khushilal to visit the town and watch the pilgrims bathe at the sacred confluence of the Bhagirathi and Alaknanda rivers. Just before crossing the suspension bridge we unexpectedly met the *sannyasi* party again. To make up time they had hired four ponies, and were now dismissing them. Moni Maharaj had recovered from his dysentery with his temper restored somewhat, but still under his vow of silence. Through one of his followers he signified that he would be grateful for the promised pills.

On our way back to the bungalow I stopped at the post office to send a telegram to Swami Ram Sarikh Singh at Badrinath, whom we were hoping to meet there. Three hours and 10 minutes later I received the answer.

Thunder was reverberating through the valley and a boisterous wind was raising clouds of dust as we left after the midday halt. Ahead of us was a steady stream of pilgrims. A little child was trying to sleep on a *panda's* shoulder, with its head bumping at every step. We made good progress as the road was level and the sun obscured, and we covered about three miles an hour. An educated pilgrim sought me out and told me he was a retired executive officer from Mysore State. He had nearly turned back when faced with the long climb out of the Hiul valley, as he feared a heart attack. Knowing the road ahead I did not discourage him by telling him there was worse to come. The talk amongst the pilgrims was about a large gang of thieves, two of whom had been caught.

I am sure it was nothing to do with the thieves, but I had a very bad night. Soon after 3 a.m. the sweeper, whose unpleasant duty it is to clean up round the *chatti*, woke everyone up to demand his '*hagg*'. There had been an attempt to carry out much needed reform, and a paternal government had ordained that pilgrims must limit their morning and evening operations to designated areas. There were separate marked areas for men and women, but rules imposed from above are often breached, and it seemed as if pilgrims got up early to outwit the sweeper, and only go to the nearest vacant spot at the edge of the road, and if caught silence the sweeper with a small gift. But the fore-mentioned sweeper had gone a step further, and was demanding a small 'tax' from every pilgrim. I felt goaded into entering into a vigorous protest, that law-abiding pilgrims might be allowed to sleep in peace. But there was nothing for it but to make an early start.

We looked forward to reaching Srinagar as the American Methodist Mission maintains a special room for guests like ourselves. But to our disappointment they had given up waiting for us and left that very morning. But the women left behind opened up the room and brought us refreshments, and Michael Dilawar, a Christian teacher from the government High School, visited us and did all he could to make us comfortable.

As we had done in 1923 we visited the famous Kamaleshwar temple, but again were not allowed beyond the limit for Christians. The priests were friendly though and posed for their photograph, and told us the legend connected with the temple. We then went on to visit the deserted temple sacred to Lakshri Narayan, that had been damaged in the Gohna flood and never restored to its full glory, and another nearby, silted up with sand. The roof looked like a rock garden with trees growing out of the tower. One small tree on top gave the impression of a feather in a hat.

As we returned through the bazaar all was quiet. The shopkeepers were observing *hartal*, news having been received that Mr Gandhi had been arrested. A heavy thunderstorm came on and continued off and on till late evening. We got very wet on our way to have supper with Balwant Singh, a Christian shopkeeper, and his wife that we had met on our previous visit, but were made very welcome and much enjoyed a well cooked meal and pleasant

Old temple damaged by Gohna flood in 1897, near Srinagar.

company. We returned the following morning for breakfast, when we were encouraged to eat to a standstill.

We decided to make an early stop at Khankra as it was a pleasant spot and the accommodation was good. We also thought the *sannyasi* party was not far behind and it would give them a chance to catch up. I went out to explore the stream and found some distance upstream a pool formed by an irrigation dam, and was able to have a good swim.

When I returned to the *chatti*, Hari Datt, a Kedarnath *panda*, was waiting to see me. I was surprised to learn that he had been present when the Ruda Ladha Ward was opened in the Friends Hospital at Itarsi. Robert Gittins, the Mission doctor, had saved his son's life, when he had found him ill with cholera, and Hari Datt had spent 11 days with him there. He intimated that he was fortunate to meet us and would count it a privilege to act as my *panda* at Kedarnath, and went on to hint that I should no doubt liberally reward him. I suggested that as his son's life had been saved at our mission hospital, the least he could do to prove his gratitude, would be to show me round Kedarnath for love. Somehow the idea did not appeal to him.

Unknown to us the *sannyasi* party had arrived after dark, and had gone on ahead while I was still trying to catch up on some sleep after most of the pilgrims had left. Compared to them I was a regular sluggard and invariably the last to leave the *chatti*. So we caught them up as they were resting after climbing out onto the ridge of a third side valley. They produced and shared some nuts, sultanas and puffed grain with us, and then we all went on together.

As it was Saturday, I intended to spend the next day as a rest day, and took advantage of the inspection bungalow at Rudraprayag. Mr Massey, the mission school master, came to welcome us, and after several other visitors had come and gone, and we had cleared up after our meal, Khushilal and I had a time of worship together out of doors. Everything was still, bathed in moonlight – only the murmur of the water rushing over the rocks in the gorge below, and the quiet little noises of insects in the trees around us. But soon the distant sound of thunder began to work its way up the valley.

After a leisurely Sunday morning we set off across the suspension bridge to call on Swami Sachchidanda, a blind *sadhu* who lives at the temple at the top of the steps leading down to the bathing place at the junction of the two rivers. Swami Sachchidanda is well known all over India, and wealthy pilgrims seek his *darshan*. He raises vast sums of money to support two schools in Devaprayag and three on the plains. He proudly told us that he had raised the money to make the concrete steps down to the water. I had noticed on our arrival at the bungalow when going to the edge of the gorge, that the natural solid slabs of rock of the promontory that I had seen in 1923 were now hidden by a hideous mass of concrete, making a solid wall on both sides of the steps. A blot on the landscape, but no doubt easier and safer for pilgrims to climb up and down.

I had been hoping for a chance to talk to Swami B. to whom I was feeling increasingly drawn. Somehow our marching times had not coincided. They caught us up at Bheri *chatti*, and I helped them find accommodation as our *chatti* was already full.

It was a beautiful moonlit night and I lay awake waiting for the moon to rise over the edge of the cliff on the opposite side of the narrow river, when I heard someone calling, 'Mr Geoffrey, Mr Geoffrey '. It was two of the *sannyasis*, one of whom I had come to

know as Mahadeo Banerjee, and with them came a beautiful hill
sheepdog. They brought a couple of little oranges – I've no idea
where they got them – and stayed for a few minutes' friendly talk
before returning to their *chatti*.

I waited for Swami B. to catch me up next morning and we
walked together to Guptkashi. I learnt that Mahadeo Banerjee and
the other old *sadhu*, Swami Atmananda, are both initiates of an old
Mahant, Bholananda, head of their sect in Hardwar. At initiation
the *guru* reads the novice's mind and gives him a suitable mantra.
The mantra gives a name of God on which the novice has to
meditate. No-one knows what mantra is given except the *guru* and
the one concerned.

We overtook a large party of well-to-do pilgrims, who, I later
discovered, came from Ghaziabad. The leader, a lawyer, Vakil
Sahib, was wearing English-style clothes and a *topi*. There was a
girl of about 15, wearing a short cotton frock and cycling stock-
ings, and several women in Indian dress. Between them they had
five *dandis*. They were picking raspberries, something ordinary
pilgrims do not do, and as I keep an eye out for them as fresh fruit
is so scarce, I was sorry that they had got to them first.

The temple at Guptkashi is surrounded on three sides by two-
storey *dharmshalas*, and swarms with *pandas* and pilgrims, so
accommodation for those not under any obligation to a *panda* is
scarce. Khushilal and I wandered up and down the street, but finally
had to give in to Swami Atmananda's request that we join them at
their *panda's* house. Khushilal was striking up a friendship with
Swami Atmananda which was very suitable as neither of them spoke
much English. Another member of the party was now under a vow
of silence and we hoped it wasn't catching.

Though we did not actually join forces, we saw the *sannyasis*
most days from now on, and I began to find out more about them.
The object of their journey was not religious, though they took the
opportunity of visiting temples and performing the usual ceremonies. They were really searching for ancient manuscripts. Moni
Maharaj was a Sanskrit scholar, so had been put in charge, though
he did not belong to the same sect as the others. Swami Atmananda
was an ex-sergeant of the Gurkha Rifles, Mahadeo Banerjee was a
Territorial in the Indian Army and an amateur heavyweight boxing
champion of Bengal. Another was a candidate who might become

high priest of Guptkashi temple and yet another hoped to become a doctor.

We tended to divide into two groups. Swami B. and Mahadeo Banerjee both spoke fluent English so I spent most of my time with them. In their company and with their support I was able to get some of the best photographs of the whole trip. Neither priests nor pilgrims raised any objections and just continued whatever they were doing. Only younger hangers-on would sometimes try to get included in the picture.

The *sannyasis* invited us to join them for their evening meal. One of their *coolies* also did all the cooking – the other, all the washing up and cleaning of pots. So after a hard day carrying loads, they had to set to and cook for eight people, for which they were paid Rs.20. each plus food. Our *coolies* only had light duties after arriving and got paid Rs.65. each, but had to find their own food. Every evening before their meal the *sannyasis* have united worship (*sandhya*), singing a long hymn, bringing in the names and attributes of Deity, and thanks for mercies during the day. The hymn has several verses and a kind of chorus, when they all bow down. The tune changes three times. Then they rise, go round and touch each other's feet and say 'Om. Namo Narayan', meaning 'I worship you as I worship the Deity'. After the meal they had a great deal of fun with one of their number who had a fit of the giggles, imitating him until they were all bordering on hysterics.

About this time I received a gentle rebuke and a lesson in *sannyasi* etiquette from Swami B. We caught up with them one morning as they were making tea and they offered us some. I declined but accepted a piece of *chapati* and a sweetmeat. Something I said made Swami B. realise I had already eaten, and I had to admit that Khushilal and I had shared some *chapati* before we left. I was told it was wrong to eat it by ourselves and that we should have shared it with them. I explained that I did not think they would be willing to eat left over food cooked by Christians. He told me that when *sannyasis* make their renunciation, such things have no meaning, and 'in future remember when we are together, you must share anything you have'.

An unusual feature just off the road in the area of Maikhanda is an enormous swing suspended from two tall pine trunks by heavy iron chains. It stands at the edge of a small open space in front of

*Swami Bishuddhananda (standing)
and Swami Atmananda (sitting)
on the great swing.*

the low-roofed ancient temple at Durga *chatti*. Once every year at a large *mela*, or religious fair, the idol is taken out of the temple and placed on the swing. The mountain villagers from many miles around assemble to witness the ceremony. On other days the swing is available for the use of pilgrims. I persuaded Swami Atmananda to sit in the swing, with Swami B. standing behind while I took their photograph.

During a particularly long steep climb in the heat of the day I noticed that Banerjee was perspiring and panting, so I relieved him of the blanket he was carrying. Back home Khushilal told me that this little incident had impressed the *sannyasis* almost more than anything else I had done.

Peaks are shy of pilgrims

Returning from the 1923 pilgrimage I had met Rev E.M. Moffatt of the Methodist Mission, who showed me a photograph he had taken of the Kedarnath temple with its backdrop of snowy peaks. It was so much better than anything I had taken, that I had set my heart on going back. I had waited seven years for the chance, and now had laid my plans to be up at Kedarnath before the clouds came down and obscured the peaks.

We spent the night at Gaurikund, seven miles of steep uphill climb short of Kedarnath. By 5 a.m. we were on the road as I reckoned it would take four hours in normal circumstances. This year great patches of snow were still lying in sheltered places and the hillsides were still snow covered. We passed a *sadhu* who had made a clever little house in a hollow tree-trunk, and several others living in artificial 'caves' by the roadside, who have inured themselves to the heat and cold. Pilgrims revere them and consider them specially holy.

Before reaching Rambara, the last *chatti* before the 3¼-mile really stiff climb to Kedarnath, we had to pass under overhanging rocks with a waterfall of melting snow. There was a great deal of snow in the river-bed forming natural bridges. Khushilal was in no hurry, so I left him chatting with fellow pilgrims and pressed on alone. I was exhilarated by the prospect and felt in good form.

I was hardly clear of the *chatti* when I saw ahead of me an old woman pilgrim. I could tell from her baggy trousers she was a Punjabi. She was going so slowly, with scarcely the energy to put one foot in front of the other in the narrow path. Every now and then she staggered, losing her balance, and had to rest leaning on her stick to regain her breath. I slowed down and watched. I knew what was ahead of her. I drew level and spoke to her. She could understand my Hindi, but I found it hard to understand her Punjabi. I gathered she had been ill (my nose told me the illness), and left behind by her relatives, who had probably got tired of waiting for her. I knew she would never make it without help.

I thought of my photograph and looked at my watch. If I stopped I would never break the record for an early arrival at Kedarnath. I slipped my hand under her arm and we began to toddle on together. We came to a long patch of snow, with a narrow single track trodden by those who had preceded us. Out of the track was a slippery slope ending on the rocks many feet below. There was only one solution. I slipped my arm round her waist, gave a heave, and tucked her comfortably under my arm. I carried her with legs dangling like a bundle of bedding and landed her safely on the other side. This operation had to be repeated several times.

A mile and a half from Kedarnath there is a dip in the hills over which it is possible to see the tip of one of the high peaks. It was still free of cloud. Time flew and we crept on. When we reached the final mile, which is on the level, and turned the corner bringing us face to face with the mountains, the peaks were completely covered by thick blankets of cloud and all hope of photography had gone for the day.

The last mile was a memorable sight. I was to learn from the *pandas* that no-one living could remember such deep snow at that time of year.

To enter Kedarnath you have to cross the river by a narrow bridge, and when we arrived there were quite a number of pilgrims, men stripped to their waists, bathing in preparation for their worship at the temple. My old lady sat and watched the bathers, and I admired their courage. Only the day before these pilgrims had taken the plunge in the hot tank at Gaurikund, and now they were bathing in water straight from the glacier only half a mile away.

It was a stiff 100-yard climb up from the river and I had brought my old lady to her destination. I took her to the centre of the town and handed her over to the *pandas* who assured me they would do what was necessary to re-unite her with her family, and I left her in their care.

The main street and some side streets had been cleared and the snow heaped up in great walls on either side. The doors of the houses and *dharmshalas* had been dug out where possible, but some were still buried up to the first floor. In due course Khushilal and four of the *sannyasi* party arrived, and in the house we eventually decided to occupy, only the upper storey was useable. From the upper-storey window I could put my hand out into the snow. I was grateful for a warm sweater under my *sadhu's* garb, but below the waist I was all goose-flesh with only a cotton garment to keep out the cold and cheap rubber-soled canvas shoes on my feet.

The snow came on again at midday, and the choice was to freeze with the shutters open or sit in darkness with them closed, and run the danger of being turned into kippers by the smoke of the cooking fires. The snow stopped towards evening after about three inches had fallen. I tried to get warm and go to sleep hoping the morning would bring better weather; but we woke to the dullest of dull days.

I had told Khushilal that I wanted to stay at least three days and do some exploring, but that was obviously going to be impossible. The *sannyasis* went to the temple and performed their worship. The *coolies* tried to persuade me to go back down as quickly as possible as they did not want to stay another night. Khushilal did not complain, but he suffers from the cold as much as I suffer from the heat and I knew he did not want to prolong the agony. So

My sannyasi friends leaving Kedarnath at midday in 1930.

there was nothing for it but to give up my photography, and I promised to spend the night back at Gaurikund.

The four *sannyasis* left at midday and I accompanied them for over half a mile, and took a photograph of them leaving as a record of their experience. I got caught in a snow storm on the way back and was thankful to return to shelter out of the cold wind. It stopped again at 3 o'clock, but still no sign of the clouds lifting.

In the meantime Swami B. had arrived with the other half of the *sannyasi* party. I packed up and sent the *coolies* off and then went to talk to Swami B. By 5 o'clock I could wait no longer. I said good-bye to Swami B. and Moni Maharaj. Half a mile outside the town I waited where I had hoped to get the picture. The clouds seemed thinner. I waited shivering in the wind for another half hour, my cotton garments flapping round my frozen limbs. Then the miracle began to happen. First a tiny rift in the clouds and a peak peeped through. I took photographs at five minute intervals, until the whole mass again stood out perfectly clear, lit by the setting sun. F.S. Smythe describing a similar happening likens it to the effect of an enormous celestial vacuum cleaner – an apt description of a wonderful and precious memory.

There was less than two hours of daylight left and I had seven miles of tricky descent ahead of me. I stopped to watch a miniature rabbit hiding among the rocks, and then again to have a word with the *sadhu* living in the hollow tree – a lonely place to spend the night. I only managed three miles in the first hour and it was dark long before I reached Gaurikund. Khushilal was too busy preparing the food to worry about my late arrival, but the *coolies* had been anxious and were about to set out to look for me with a lantern.

The finest view in Garhwal

Back at Bhenta we went to pick up our surplus luggage from the old man who provides this service for the pilgrims on their way up to Kedarnath. We offered him a present for his trouble, but he refused and offered instead to give us some food. It is not the custom to accept money for this service. We went on to Nala for breakfast, but the firewood was so damp we had to give up the idea of *chapatis* and lentils, and make do with *kichari*. A *pujari* boy from the temple tried to persuade me to have the *darshan*. I tried to explain that that was not my idea of worship, and persuade him to buy one of my books so he would understand. Though the price was only a farthing, he was determined to bargain with me. Finally he crushed me with, 'Fancy such a big man as you bothering about half a farthing'.

I hoped to find another friendly Indian doctor at Ukhimath hospital, and I was not disappointed. Dr Gajendra Thapa could not let us have the same room as in 1923, as he had cases of cholera and smallpox to isolate, but did give us a room higher up the hillside, near a little stream. This suited admirably as I was able to develop some films. The water looked crystal clear, but must have contained fine particles of mica which I could not later remove.

Dr Thapa came to my room to chat when he could spare the time and I asked him about the cholera outbreak the previous year. At least 1,000 pilgrims had died. The pilgrims do the best they can to care for each other, but the *coolie* hillmen desert the sick as soon as an epidemic breaks out. It's impossible to dispose of the corpses, so they are pushed over the edge down the mountainside and are devoured by jackals and vultures. The government is reluctant to stop a pilgrimage, as the loss to shopkeepers and others financially interested causes hardship, and the pilgrims themselves consider it unwarranted interference in their religious practice. The doctors have no authority to detain pilgrims suffering from cholera, so the infection rapidly spreads down the watercourses.

On the terraced hillside inside the hospital compound is a row of tombs. For 300 years the Rawals of Kedarnath have been buried here. There are a dozen tombs, like small temples averaging eight feet in height, each with a small *lingam* inside, representing the god Shiva. The oldest stands by itself under a small tree, and it is sacred to the memory of a Rawal who died about 300 years ago and whose wife committed *suttee*. The doctor told me there were even earlier tombs down by the river, but I did not see them. There is something beautiful about the last resting place of the Rawals of Kedarnath, and the great Kedarnath peak seems to be keeping a watchful eye on this peaceful spot.

Shaivite Hindus, said to be in the majority, consider Kedarnath a more holy and important place than Badrinath. Dr Thapa maintained that Kedarnath represented a spirit that is superior to material things, whereas Badrinath was wealthier and more materialistic. My own experience of both places confirms this impression, which made it easier to believe.

Dr Thapa took me to visit the present Rawal Sahib who lives in Ukhimath during the winter, goes up to open the Kedarnath temple when the snow has melted sufficiently for it to be approached, but only moves up to stay in Kedarnath when the weather becomes warmer. The temple and flagged courtyard is surrounded by substantial two-storey buildings, and approached up a flight of steps to a lofty gateway with massive wooden doors. The temple is typical of the style of this area, with the roof of the tower covered with gold sheets. Here they have a black stone idol of Raja Mandhata, whose miraculous birth is described in the Banparva section of the Mahabharata.

The Rawal, like all previous Rawals of Kedarnath belongs to the Nambudri caste of Brahmans from South India – the sect to which Shankaracharya belonged. He was dressed in saffron-coloured clothes similar to mine, and sitting on a rug by an open window looking over the town and across the valley to Guptkashi. He told me about the boys' schools, Sanskrit and Ayurvedic schools he maintained on the Plains. Speaking of the pilgrimage he said many people thought that Shankaracharya had founded it, whereas in fact he had only revived it – it was a very ancient institution.

From Ukhimath the road zig-zags round the hillside in a long steep climb. Most pilgrims were well ahead of me but I overtook the man who had been in the hospital suffering from smallpox. He was recovering, but the old lady with him travelling in a *kandi* on the *coolie's* back had the full-blown disease. I was sorry for the *coolie* and did not linger.

I had been compelled to turn back when only a mile and a half from Tungnath on my last pilgrimage, by an unbearable pain in my chest, so I was anxious to try again this time. It was just getting light as we set off, a clear sky gave every hope that we would see 'the finest view in Garhwal' from the 14,000 feet peak. My hands were stiff with cold, but the strenuous effort demanded by the ascent soon brought the circulation back. The path had been considerably improved. All the way up tempting views presented themselves, especially of Chaukhamba, and I wished I had more film. Several mauve rhododendrons were in flower – too big for bushes, and scarcely big enough to be called trees like the red variety. A mile below the temple, on a conspicuous corner, is the 'last tree' – a gaunt weather-beaten pine, with mossy limbs. Beyond that the gradient is easier and the path runs parallel with the ridge, cutting across slopes of tufted grass. It's quite a shock to discover that you are actually on half a mountain – the other side of the ridge is a sheer precipice.

On reaching the temple, the first object of interest is the bathing tank. There is no spring, but the water that trickles through the brass cow's mouth comes directly from a great patch of snow in a sheltered north-facing depression. A few pilgrims were bathing and drying their clothes around the tank and we soon found a quiet upper room for ourselves in the Kalikamliwala's *dharmshala*.

The altitude is higher than at Kedarnath and I felt breathless. Many pilgrims experience this and do not understand the cause. We pressed on, though, as our prime objective was to see the view from the summit. Tungnath stands well away from other smaller peaks, so you seem to be standing almost in space, at the centre of a semi-circle of the grandest snowy peaks in the world. For the pilgrim it is the three groups nearest him, Badrinath, Kedarnath and Gangotri, that claim his attention; and on this occasion they were at their very best. We spent half an hour at the summit and by 9 o'clock clouds had covered the bigger peaks.

The *sannyasi* party and the Vakil Sahib and his party arrived at Tungnath during the day, and both parties asked me to photograph them as a record of their being in such a sacred place. Instead of payment the Vakil asked me to share their meal, cooked by the women, and quite substantial. Later when the *sannyasis* asked me to share their meal after photographing them, I had to confess I had already eaten, but they would not accept that as an excuse, and I managed to put away four more *puris*. Meanwhile Khushilal and the *coolies* had already started down. Swami B. accompanied me a little way, relieving his mind by telling me of his troubles with Moni Maharaj, who had decided to stay three nights at Tungnath when he knew all they wanted was to get down to lower altitudes away from the severe cold as soon as possible.

A new six-foot wide path was being cut on the descent, and the most difficult and dangerous part had already been completed, so progress was rapid. Several people caught me up and praised the government for this improvement. The area so reminded me of Kashmir, I was thinking it was strange that I had not met a single *sadhu* who recognised me as being on the Amarnath pilgrimage the previous year, when the very next *sadhu* I overtook told me he had met me there. Rejoining Khushilal I had to eat yet another breakfast, but thanks to a five-mile walk and the descent of several thousand feet, I was able to show him how much I appreciated his labour of love.

Gopeshwar is less well known, but still important enough to be the seat of a Rawal Sahib. Dr Thapa had told me that the Rawal I had visited in 1923 had been deposed (I gathered that he had worshipped mammon rather than God), and the new man was a 'good man', and that I should make his acquaintance. Had it not been for this I would not have stopped at Gopeshwar as I had seen it all last time. When I enquired I found the Rawal was in the same room from which I had hurriedly been asked to withdraw. I sent in my card and was told the Rawal was ready to see me. I stood in the doorway and enquired if I might enter as I was a Christian. He replied that any worshipper of God, be he Hindu, Christian or Moslem, was welcome. So we went in and he asked us to sit near him on the floor.

At first he was polite, but very soon asked questions about my saffron coloured clothes implying that I was an impostor and deceiver. I told him that I had long ago surrendered my life to the service of God, and so had as much right to wear the clothes as he or any other *sadhu* had. He then started flinging quotations in Sanskrit at me, which he knew I did not understand, and so could not follow his argument, let alone reply. Khushilal, a Sanskrit scholar himself, and from his knowledge of the Hindu scriptures, was able to produce a suitable quotation stating that in ancient times it was allowable for anyone to wear coloured cloth.

I was aware that other people had come into the room and sat down behind us. I find it a trial that any conversation with important people in India has to be conducted in public. I dislike being called a deceiver at the best of times and it's even more unpleasant when the accusation is made in front of an unknown number of people whom you cannot see. I made no attempt to answer back, but left it to Khushilal who seemed to be coping well. The Rawal became more heated, and frustrated, shifting his ground and angle of attack. He asked me how we served God, and I replied we served Him through service to our fellow men. He maintained we should not serve bad men as this meant satisfying their evil desires. He also denied the necessity of preaching as a man who had found God would attract others to him. Khushilal reminded him that the pilgrimage was a vast illustration contradicting what he had said, as the whole organisation depended on the propaganda carried out by the *pandas* on the plains during the cold weather, scouring India persuading people to come on the pilgrimage. There was a general murmur of agreement from those behind us. Gradually the Rawal cooled down and when he seemed to have reached a point at which we could retire without appearing to be running away, we took our leave.

As we rose the audience rose with us and followed us downstairs into the temple courtyard and out into the street. I was expecting to feel hostility and scorn as one publicly disgraced, but they were cordial and friendly. When we were alone Khushilal explained that the *pandas* considered that I had come out best from the encounter as I had kept my temper, whereas the Rawal had lost his and been rude to his visitors.

A few days later we met a *sadhu* who had been listening to our conversation with the Rawal. Some of the things we had said had fallen on good ground, and after talking with him we gave him several Scripture portions.

'Sit underneath the bed'

From Gopeshwar, a long easy descent into the Alaknanda valley brings us to Chamoli. As in other larger places there are no *chattis* with their attendant shop-keepers. As we had become separated from the *sannyasi* party and had no permit, we did not expect the caretaker of the Kalikamliwala's *dharmshala* to accept us, but he raised no objections and gave us a room. More pilgrims avoiding the *pandas* arrived and soon it was pretty crowded and we were unable to spread out our bedding for a proper rest. So, rather reluctantly, that afternoon we walked on through Math *chatti* with its shady *peepul* trees and spring from which it is safe to drink, and pressed on to the next *chatti*, a four-mile climb ahead. I noticed Khushilal seemed slow and tired, and found he had an attack of malaria. We found a *chatti* which we had to ourselves, and cooked some coarse white radishes that Khushilal had bought at Math *chatti*, with onions and the everlasting lentils, though Khushilal did not feel much like eating. The Vakil's party were nearby and I talked with him at length on the Vedanta, in which he is a firm believer.

It was hard to get going the next day. I was tired and Khushilal more so. We were soon overtaken by Mahadeo Banerjee and his companions, feeling fit and in good form. Much later we caught them up again as they sat chatting to a shopkeeper and they shared some *jalebi* with us. After a rest we paired off, Banerjee walking with me, and Swami Atmananda with Khushilal. We had been meeting large numbers of old women with shaven heads for several days. Being a Bengali, Banerjee recognised them as Bengali widows. Many such women congregate at sacred places all over India, where charitable organisations provide them with food, and this year they must have decided to do the pilgrimage. Banerjee told me of a girl he knew who married at the age of 13, and eight days later became a widow. Widows are not allowed even a drop of water on *ekadasi* (the 11th day of a lunar fortnight) although the rest of the family have specially good food on that day. He had taken part in a debate at the YMCA in Calcutta, and got thrown out by his fellow Hindus for advocating the re-marriage of widows. We also discussed the question of *swaraj*. He longed for it, but felt that social and moral reform ought to come first.

Once more under the wing of the *sannyasis* we shared their privilege of private rooms in the Kalikamliwala's *dharmshala*, where a large *darri* was provided for resting on the floor. After I had had as much sleep as the flies allowed I got up and made a cup of tea for myself and anyone else who wanted it. I reflected on the curious assortment of companions among which a Quaker had fallen, and if I had met no-one else, it was surely worthwhile joining such an interesting group.

I made friends with a *sadhu* who had been to Gangotri before joining the main body of pilgrims at Trijugi Narayan. He told of the hardships of that road owing to snow covering the track. They had come across a woman almost exhausted, tried to help her, but had finally had to leave her to die. In his youth he had met a missionary on a train who had given him a Gospel portion. He remembered Christ's teaching: 'if you are asked to sit on a *charpoy*, sit underneath it'. I gave him three portions in Urdu, and several other *sadhus* who had been sitting listening asked for books, and I gave them the Gospel of Mark in Hindi.

We enquired for Ajab Singh as we past Jharkula *chatti*, and heard that he was still around, but we did not get an opportunity to seek him out again.

This time we stopped at Pandukeshwar. The twin temples simply asked to be photographed. They are picturesque in themselves and framed by steep rocky cliffs on either side with a snowy peak in the background. Khushilal and four of our *sannyasi* friends provide the human interest and complete the picture. Both the temples are served by one priest, who by tradition must be a pure Brahman from South India. In one temple there is said to be a beautiful metal image of the god Vishnu, splendidly ornamented with precious stones, and in the other a metal image of Vasudevji, also very ornate. Only the priest is allowed to enter, and even Hindu pilgrims have to make their obeisance from the outside.

At this altitude the road passes through pleasant forest. Horse chestnuts in full bloom overhung the road, and the white wild roses were at their best. Walking with Banerjee, he told me how he had experienced 'indescribable joy' when he embraced the *lingam*

Pandukeshwar, Khushilal and some of the sannyasi party, 1930.

(emblem of Shiva) in the temple at Kedarnath. He earnestly longed to go back there again taking his wife and family members with him. He had not wanted to marry, but had yielded to his father's persuasions. He had been married five years and had a son, who had died. He owns a rice-mill which brings in sufficient to support himself and his wife, so he is free to adopt the religious life. His parents, who are wealthy, have willed their money at his request for God's work, so that he will not become entangled in worldly affairs.

A tea-party becomes a Sacrament

I had been looking forward to occupying the inspection bungalow at Badrinath and having three nights in a bed. I had the required permit and had ascertained that no government official was likely to be wanting to occupy it. So it was a blow to discover the place all locked up and that the caretaker lived at Lambagar, which we had passed through the previous day, a good seven miles back down the hill.

For Khushilal and myself the chief attraction of Badrinath was Swami Ram Sarikh Singh, whose acquaintance we had made in 1923, and with whom I had kept up an intermittent correspondence. We met a *sadhu* (who turned out to be a learned Vedanta

scholar), who kindly undertook to guide us to the Swami's cottage
– help we appreciated as, though quite close, it was hard to find
among the many others on a terrace above the rocky banks of the
river directly opposite the temple.

Ram Sarikh Singh was as overjoyed to see us as we were to see
him. He welcomed us into his little front room, spread rugs to sit
on, and brought more rugs to wrap ourselves in. He made tea and
preparations for food which were most acceptable before arrang-
ing for someone to go and tell the caretaker of our arrival. Then he
told us all the local news. He had decided to part company with
the temple authorities and the Kalikamliwalas, as they resented his
outspoken way of drawing attention to the many abuses that bring
the pilgrimage into disrepute.

Back at the bungalow we were relieved to find the kitchen, a
small separate building, was not locked and there was just sufficient space to spread out our bedding. A clear spring nearby provided us with drinking water and just behind the bungalow a
good-sized pond of melted snow provided all our washing needs.

I found myself torn between conflicting loyalties to my old
friend Ram Sarikh Singh on our side of the river, and to my new
sannyasi friends in the town on the other. Each remonstrated with
me for neglect if I was with the other. So I invited the *sannyasis* to
come over to our side of the river so that we could all have tea
together. I was apprehensive as to how they would get on together.
Seven years before I had felt that RSS was one of whom Christ
would have said, 'Thou art not far from the Kingdom of God'.
Since then he had made the break with Hinduism. Here, in the
holiest place of all, he had tried Hinduism and found it wanting,
but was not yet quite ready to call himself a Christian.

It was a pleasant sunny afternoon as we gathered out of doors,
sheltered from the wind. The *sannyasis* in their saffron robes arrived
first, then RSS in his long brown woollen robe, reaching his ankles.
Time passed quickly and after tea RSS made a little speech, referring to our friendship in sincere but too complimentary terms I
felt, and then went on to say, 'It is Mr Maw who has invited us to
come here this afternoon, but he has come as a representative of
Jesus Christ, so it is really Jesus Christ's tea-party, and it is at His
invitation that we have come together'. And so it was RSS who

made us feel that the tea-party had become a sacrament and the mountains around Badrinath the hills of Galilee.

The most striking feature in the area is the beautiful snowy peak of Nalikanta, or sometimes Nilkanth, which stands at the head of the Rishiganga valley. From the verandah of the bungalow the view of the peak is breathtaking, and lit by the moon or the rising sun, is an unforgettable sight. No wonder the Hindus believe the god Vishnu dwells there.

Pilgrim's footwear is not suited to mountaineering, but I had to see how far up the valley I could get. I suggested the *sannyasis* should take half a day off from their devotions and join me. Almost immediately outside the town there is a stiff climb of several hundred feet, after which the slope is more gradual. Here the ground was dotted with wild iris, blue and purple. The *sannyasis* had soon had enough, and decided to return, while Khushilal humoured my roving instinct, and we went on until our sandals could no longer provide a grip in the snow, and we had to return.

An evening spent with RSS developed naturally into a time of worship 'after the manner of Friends'. Referring to prayer that had been offered out of the silence, RSS said 'I wish I could speak to God as Father like you do. I know Him and speak to Him as God, but I cannot yet speak to Him as Father'. We spoke of the revelation of the Father through the Son, and I suggested that the truth could only be found by experiment, and that he should try taking Christ as his *guru*, following his teaching as an Indian *chela* would follow his *guru*; and not worry about problems he could not yet understand, as these would solve themselves. As he came to know Jesus by experience and believe in Him, he would experience God as his Father.

The Source at Last

For seven long years I had planned for the day I could set out again to reach Alkapuri, the source of the Alaknanda. It was now or never. I hoped that Khushilal and I would be allowed to have the day to ourselves, to make an early start and travel quickly. But our *sannyasi* friends had other ideas as they wanted to come too, not only to see the source but also the famous Basudhara Falls. So it became an expedition, with a local guide and provisions and other paraphernalia in a *kandi*.

When we arrived before 7 a.m. at the *sannyasis'* lodgings there was no sign of imminent departure. So there was nothing for it but to abandon all care as to whether the mountains were going to disappear in cloud at 9 o'clock, and just enjoy it. It was certainly a glorious morning and the air was exhilarating.

Dear old Swami Atmananda had the dignified gait of an elephant – this is a compliment in India – and etiquette demands that all stick together until someone expresses the desire not to go further. The path was good and level to Mana village, but after crossing the roaring Sarsuti tributary by the natural rock bridge, the path fades to practically nothing – the further you go the rougher and steeper it becomes. We seemed to creep up the interminable slope, but at last reached the high ground where we had stopped in 1923 and from which I had thought I had seen the source. Off to the right we could see the thin white line of the Basudhara falls, 700 feet high, looking like a white thread against the cliff. Was it this that was in the mind of the author of the Skanda Purana when he wrote, 'where the Ganges falls from the foot of Vishnu like the slender thread of a lotus flower?'

We pressed on, threading our way between rocks and came upon a small pond in which the surrounding mountains were reflected – an excellent place to stop though I desperately wanted to go on. So far the weather was holding though it was well after 9 o'clock. Swami Atmananda stretched himself out in the sun, and by this time we were all hungry, so it was decided to have breakfast. The *sannyasis* had seen to it that there was no lack; *puris*, potato and vegetable curries and plenty of sweets. The *sannyasis* were at peace with the world and all their desire to reach the source evaporated. If we wanted to go on, we were welcome to do so and we parted company. It was the opportunity I had been hoping for and Khushilal and I got to our feet.

Straight away we encountered difficulties. Between us and the source lay two miles of loose boulders and no trace of a path or smooth soft spots to put our feet. Then disaster struck – jumping from one boulder to another Khushilal slipped, tried to save himself with his precious iron-tipped hill stick, but it jammed between the rocks and snapped. What was left was some use, but it made it much more difficult for him. Then we came upon an unexpected stream, invisible until we were almost upon it, as the water was the same colour as the rocks. It came from a glacier in a side valley, not very deep but too swift to wade through and icy cold. At last after going further up the hillside we found a place where we could cross safely.

I did not realise how lucky we were until I read Frank S. Smythe's account of his adventures at this spot in *Kamet Conquered*. He was there in July 1931, just 14 months after us. Here is his description, from chapter XXIII:

> 'We entered a stony waste of waterworn boulders, washed down from the mouth of a side valley by spring floods. This valley contained a glacier, and as we suspected, the glacier discharged a torrent of formidable size. We had been following a rude track to the edge of the stones, and hoped, there fore, to find a bridge across the torrent, but when we came to it, not only could we find no bridge, but we experienced grave misgivings as to the possibility of fording it. The mists had closed down upon us, and as it was impossible to see far, Greene ascended the bank of the torrent in search of a bridge or a snowdrift, while I looked for a ford. The torrent was a steep one, and its waters tumultuous. In one place it was divided into two by a bank of boulders, and, as it was slightly less steep here, there seemed a chance of fording it. Presently, when Greene returned unsuccessful, we determined to try to effect a crossing. I went first, with a rope tied round my waist, held from the bank upstream, so that it would be of maximum assistance in preventing me from being washed off my feet. The depth of the torrent was not more than three feet, but what it lacked in depth it made up for in steepness and energy, and even with a rope it was all I could do to avoid being torn from my foothold. Greene followed likewise tied to a rope. Now that we had a handrail of rope stretched across, there seemed no need for each of the porters to be roped separately; the hand rail should suffice to prevent them from being swept from their feet.
>
> The Old Soldier came next, carrying my tent, sleeping bag and other equipment. Although ungainly in appearance, his strength is prodigious, and he crossed with scarcely a pause, a broad grin on his face. Our old friend the Egg-wallah followed, carrying our box of provisions on his back. For a few yards he went well. He crossed one branch of the torrent to the central bank of boulders, and essayed the other. He would have been alright had he gone quickly, but he hesitated in the worst part of the torrent when he was about two yards from the bank. For a few moments he struggled to maintain his foothold, but the torrent was too strong for him, and though he clung tightly to the rope, he was swept from his feet. Even then had he kept his wits about him, he could have reached the bank, by

pulling himself along the rope, but instead clung helplessly to the rope petrified with fear. It was all over in a second or two. In an instant he disappeared into the raging waters. He reappeared a few yards lower down on the edge of a vertical fall, quite 10 feet, and vanished over it; before we had time to think, he was dashed over a lower fall, then another and another. It was a terrible spectacle. For a moment we paused, horrified, then raced down the bank, leaping from boulder to boulder. It seemed certain he must perish, dashed into pulp on the rocks, and we had given up all hope, when to our amazement we saw him crawl slowly out of a pool.

Greene was the first to reach him. At the best we expected to find many broken bones, but an examination disclosed nothing worse than severe bruising, and superficial cuts. His escape had been a miraculous one, for he had been carried about a hundred yards down a raging torrent through a vertical height of at least forty to fifty feet, and over a series of falls up to fifteen feet each in height. The poor old man's clothes had been torn from him with the exception of his shirt, and he was groaning and shivering in an excess of terror and cold.'

It was slow and painful walking over the boulders. Coming down towards us on our left was the Satopanth glacier, and behind it the incomparable Chaukhamba with its four peaks. Straight ahead was Kunaling with the Bhagat Kharah glacier coming in on its right.

As we got closer and looked up the Satopanth glacier we saw the other side of Nalikanta. If only I had known, this was the valley up which we should have gone to find the source. In any case we had neither the strength nor the time if we were to return that day. It was some time later that I realised I had again missed my chance of reaching the source.

We struggled along for another hour and a half and reached what I had thought was the source – the little black spot amongst the boulders directly below the peak of Kunaling, but on reaching the black cliff it was nothing but a bare wall of ice, and the river took a sharp turn out of a cup-shaped depression with very steep sides, which had been hidden from us. The boulders started to give way under our weight, sliding towards the water and we had to jump quickly from one to another. On the opposite side, the boulders came down almost to the water's edge where there was a foot-wide shelf of solid ice under which the water burst out with tremendous force. This was what I had mistakenly thought was the source.

Though tired we had no time to rest and started back imme-
diately, pausing only to eat a few sultanas and groundnuts that
Khushilal had thoughtfully brought. With only four hours of day-
light left I calculated that we were at least seven miles from
Badrinath and would be doing well if we managed a mile an hour.
It would be dark long before we got back.

I had several opportunities on the way back of seeing the
Basudhara Fall. I was a bit contemptuous of it. The mountain sides
are so vast as they tower into the sky, and I wondered why Hindus
held it in such reverence. Suddenly I had to stop and stare and
never since have I been contemptuous of Basudhara. A sudden gust
of wind struck the fall; the lower half changed from a thin thread
into a sheet of glistening spray; then the whole stream was taken
and dispersed so that none of it reached the ground. It was so beautiful it took my breath away.

In spite of my fears the day had been cloudless until I had taken
all my photographs, but now white clouds had gathered, and by
the time we reached the pond where we had had our breakfast with
the *sannyasis*, were being replaced by ominous storm clouds coming
up behind us and ahead over Mana village. We tried to quicken our
steps, but were tired and the path was too rough to hurry. As we
turned south for the last two miles to Badrinath we left the storm
clouds behind, and arrived just as it got dark. As we came to the
temple the *bhog* was being distributed, and crowds of hurrying
sadhus were pushing and scrambling taking away as much as they
could grab in both hands; we were back in the real world. The final
climb up to the bungalow from the bridge seemed the last straw.
We were both as near done in as ever I can remember.

Frank Smythe with a well-equipped expedition had camped
beyond Mana, not far from where we had our breakfast, and had
returned after reaching the source for another night before returning to Badrinath. We had added on at least another two miles at
either end and done it in a day, so it was not surprising that we were
exhausted.

A *Sannyasi's* Vision of Christ

We took things easy the next day. I had tea with RSS at his little
cottage overlooking the temple, aware of the constant stream of
worshippers across the river as they tolled the great bell in the
temple gateway to draw the attention of the god to their arrival.

We spoke together of what RSS called two mysteries. First, some time previously he had arranged to read the Vedas in the original with a Sanskrit scholar from Rishikesh. He had not arrived and we had come instead – there must be some purpose in it. The second mystery, our visit to Badrinath that particular year. He said, 'I believe that God brought you here on my account'. He no longer had any faith in *gurus* or their initiation, but said my suggestion to take Christ as his *guru* had been like an initiation to him. The conversation turned to the manner of Quaker worship, which I explained as fully as possible, and the evening ended with prayer and silent worship together.

The day of our departure had arrived. We packed in good time and started the *coolies* off by 7 a.m. Then I went on a round of farewells. First to find the *sannyasis'* Bengali *panda*, Ram Prasad, who had been very attentive and helpful, and chose to have a certificate for services rendered signed by me rather than money, and I had no difficulty in writing a *chit* that was truthful, and I hope of value to him. As we said goodbye he asked to be mentioned in my book – so here he is: Ram Prasad Suraj Prasad, Panch Bhai, Pandas, Devaprayag.

Khushilal then started off down the hill to join the *coolies*, while I joined RSS for a cup of tea and pistachio nuts. Back over the river Swami B. came with me to try and get the promised interview with the Rawal, but he 'was not feeling well'. Then to the bazaar to visit my friend Govind Prasad, a bookseller from Nandprayag, who runs the largest shop in Badrinath, selling souvenirs and photographic picture postcards, made from photographs that I took in 1923. I had given him the copyright which had helped to pay some of my expenses, and I hoped I might be able to do another deal with him. Back to RSS's cottage for a final meal which he had cooked himself. I made a special note of ' potato in soup', not potato soup, followed by *chapatis* with curried sultanas. For the last time I watched the pilgrims going up and down the stone steps from the temple to the hot spring, and listened to the clamour of the crowd as they bathed and washed their clothes. As the bell clanged, like the tolling of a funeral bell, I wondered how many of them had found what they had come to seek.

It was hard to tear myself away. Would it be another seven years before I would be back? Khushilal had three hours' start on me

*In 1930 Khushilal left Badrinath three hours before me, and when I came
to cross this bridge it had gone.*

and I had no time to linger. I stopped to photograph a temple attendant tending the shrine to Ganesh, where the pilgrims get their first
glimpse of Badrinath. Scarcely had I parted from him when I saw
an old lady staggering up the hill. To my great joy I discovered it
was 'my old Punjabi woman'. She was overjoyed to see me and put
her arms around me in the Hindustani embrace. It had been 15
days since I left her at Kedarnath, and she was still alone, had
covered 108 miles, and seemed stronger than when I last saw her.

   With the worst of the descent behind me I discovered that the
bridge had been washed away and there was nothing but a rushing
torrent. It was a shock to realise I was on the wrong side of the river
and Khushilal, my breakfast, the *coolies* and the luggage were somewhere down the valley in blissful ignorance. However, I soon found
out that there was a snow bridge half a mile back, and pilgrims were
already going round that way. I retraced my steps to a big patch of
snow, so thick that the sound of the torrent beneath could not be
heard, and over it the beginnings of a track made by those who had
crossed before me. The track led out onto a 200-yard landslide

which had not yet finished slipping; showers of stones and occasional bigger lumps came bouncing down as I gingerly crept along a very insecure new track, trying not to think of the foaming river 30 feet below. In the middle I met an old woman pilgrim being assisted across by two *coolies*. She had been travelling in a *kandi*, but even these sure-footed *coolies* felt it too risky to carry her pick-a-back across the landslide.

When I caught up with Khushilal and the *coolies* I learnt that when Khushilal had arrived at the bridge, it was almost awash and looked very shaky, but he and others had crossed it safely.

Since leaving Badrinath we had come under pressure of time in which to get back to Hardwar. I was reluctant to leave the *sannyasis* but they seemed in no hurry and Moni Maharaj was being perverse, stopping when the others wanted to go on. Swami B. suggested that the only way to persuade him to co-operate was to flatter him about his cooking. I put his theory to the test, by telling him I had a craving for mango chutney and had heard that unripe mangoes could be obtained at Rudraprayag. (He was justly famed for his mango chutney.) Before the others were even ready to start he was off down the road as if he had to catch the last bus home.

We caught Moni Maharaj up at Pipalkoti and as Khushilal was reluctant to go further without a rest, I decided to see if I could find somewhere to bathe. I succeeded far beyond my expectations. A short scramble through some terraced fields brought me to a cliff, with a shady clear pool at the foot of a waterfall, deep enough to lie down in. Afterwards I sat on a rock and had a hunt among my clothing for those little creatures that prey on unsuspecting travellers.

I returned in time for the afternoon march and to my dismay found Khushilal had a high temperature. The *coolie* put it down to our eating some unripe greengages earlier, but on that theory I ought to have had a much worse fever!

I felt it was better to try and make some progress, however slow, as we were 10 miles from the nearest hospital at Chamoli. With frequent stops it took us all afternoon to reach the next *chatti*. There was no suitable upstairs accommodation, so we had to be content with a crowded ground floor room. Though Khushilal was far from well, I remembered what had happened in similar circumstances in 1923. I waited till the pilgrims had quietened down, and then I knelt by Khushilal as he lay on the ground. In the quietness he was instantaneously healed and got up and offered to make my bedding ready for the night. When we lay down he was restless at first, but later slept peacefully.

Swami B. not far away, was also feeling unwell in the night, and woke Madho, their Brahman *coolie*/cook, to come and massage him. I looked at my watch; it was ten minutes past three. I got a little more sleep but we were all up and off before 4.35 a.m. Khushilal was quite his old self again and a pain in his knee which had been troubling him for some days had also gone. The tables had turned; it was now I who could not keep up with him even on the downhill.

I had not intended to tell Swami B. what had happened, but as it was obvious that Khushilal was so much better, I hesitantly told him what had happened the previous evening, and instead of doubting my story, he took me by surprise by saying, 'I have been feeling very unwell lately, I wish you would have a time of prayer with me'. That night by putting our best foot forward we reached Nandprayag and as agreed Swami B. shared our room. It was a large upper room, with a low roof and I had to be careful not to crack my head on the beams. Khushilal and I settled down at one end and the *sannyasis* at the other. When all was quiet Swami B. joined us. I explained what I would do, and said that I hoped during the time of worship he would also pray for his own healing. We sat cross-legged on a blanket and shortly I knelt in front of Swami B. and put my hands on his shoulders and prayed that he might be healed in the name of Christ. After a short period of silence our meeting 'broke up', and we prepared our bedding for the night.

I woke at 4 a.m. disturbed by the bustle of the departure of the *sannyasi* party. Swami B. seeing I was awake told me he felt very much better, the pains had gone and so had his cold. We started later and caught them up. Naturally our conversation soon came round to spiritual healing. Swami B. remarked that if we had faith in any saint, whether it be the Lord Christ or the Lord Krishna, we were bound to get benefit by it.

When later Swami B. next overtook me, he told me the full story of what really happened the previous evening. While he was sitting praying he had a clear vision of Christ on the Cross, and again this morning while resting in the cool shade, the vision had returned. He had tried to take his mind off it, but it had persisted, and he said, 'even now, as I am walking, I can see it'. He admitted that even in his student days at the Scottish Mission College in Calcutta, he 'used to meditate on the name of Christ'.

Far below us, the river was spotted with railway sleepers, floating down stream to be gathered at Hardwar. Many had been caught up in eddies or jammed among rocks, and men were at work dislodging them; pushing them out into the current. The men were floating on *masaks*, inflated buffalo skins, which floated tummy side up, with the leg stumps in the air, and they propelled them lying on their tummies and kicking out with their legs behind.

Au Revoir

It was my turn to treat the whole *sannyasi* party. Moni Maharaj agreed to make the arrangements and do the cooking. My part was to pay the bill. I discovered that this time, his motivation was not so much to show off his cooking, as to show how much he could eat. Brahmcharya, the candidate among them for the priesthood, explained in an aside, that this was one of the ways Moni Maharaj's vanity expressed itself. He had been caught cheating on previous occasions; giving his food to dogs and even going outside and making himself sick. I suspected he hoped I would take up his challenge, but I had no intention of allowing him to demonstrate his superiority over me by competing.

Moni Maharaj was still being capricious, starting before light and then dawdling over a long hot midday rest, and we had to keep reminding him of the unripe mangoes, so good for mango chutney, at Rudraprayag. When we did arrive at Rudraprayag, Khushilal and I went to the PWD bungalow, where Mr Massey, the mission school teacher, had a meal all ready for us. The *sannyasis* were to stay in the school compound, but soon after arriving, Moni Maharaj decided differently and gave orders to march two miles further on to the next *chatti*.

I was expecting the next morning's march to be a long one, and we were later in starting not having the *sannyasis* to get us up early. There were the three ridges to cross with equally steep descents on the other side, but we managed them easily. The *sannyasis* had had a two-mile start and we saw nothing of them till we overtook them leaving their *chatti* in the afternoon. Moni Maharaj was suffering another attack of dysentery and was walking very slowly. We continued with them to Srinagar, having done rather more than 19 miles during the day, settled them in the *dharmshala* and ourselves on the verandah of the Mission House, before returning with the dysentery tablets for Moni Maharaj. As I settled down for the night I saw an enormous black scorpion creeping down the wall a couple of feet from my head. I picked up one of my sandals and terminated his pilgrimage.

I had a surprise the following day when we were stopped by a pony boy coming up the road. He had found the keys of my Kashmiri *kiltas* that I had lost five weeks previously, and kept them expecting to see me again sooner or later.

We arrived in good time at Umrasu where we intended to spend the night. The *sannyasis* had taken a sudden spurt and gone on ahead. We chose a convenient empty *chatti*, cooked and ate our evening meal in peace, and prepared to settle down early and have a good rest. The peace was shattered when a Hindu *zamindar* with his party and several servants decided to share our upper floor. The *zamindar* was noisy and ostentatious, angry with his servants over trifles, and shouted at all who annoyed him. We tried to ignore them. One of them started to do violent physical exercises which shook the floor. A *charpoy* was found for the *zamindar* and two servants proceeded to massage him from head to toe, and finally his lordship had to have the soles of his feet tickled, which caused much giggling but eventually had a soothing effect and he fell peacefully asleep. The poor servants then had to repeat the treatment on lesser members of the party. All this time dogs were barking in the narrow street below. Twice I got up to try and put a stop to the noise, but it only made matters worse. A far from peaceful night.

Throughout the trip I had been troubled by pain in my hip, not only when walking, but also at night sleeping on the floor with only the thickness of a couple of blankets underneath. I had hoped that an opportunity would arise when Khushilal could pray for my healing, but something like the arrival of the *zamindar's* party always seemed to intervene. Our last night arrived and we found a peaceful spot away from the pilgrims among great smooth boulders near the river to sit and meditate. After a time of silence Khushilal told me he did not feel at liberty to lay hands on me, and that if it was God's will for me to be healed through prayer, there was no need for anyone to intervene. After some further talk together, we returned to the *chatti*, and as it promised to be a fine night, we lay down in the open under the stars.

Wednesday, 11th June, our last morning on the road arrived. Khushilal celebrated by making a most successful pudding for *chhoti haziri* from last night's left-over rice, some drinking chocolate, the remnant of the Klim milk powder and some sultanas. With this foundation we soon covered the remaining four miles to Lachhman Jhula and were once more back in civilisation. While doing some business at the Post Office at Rishikesh, I was conscious of being watched by a group of young men wearing Gandhi caps and *kheddar* clothes. They approached me and wanted to know who I was and what I was doing wearing Indian dress. They accused me of trying to deceive people, and as usual other people gathered around to listen. To my amazement the crowd was friendly, and an old Hindu gave me a kindly pat on the shoulder and made me feel among friends.

Sitting in the motor lorry between Rishikesh and Hardwar it did feel as if we were returning from another world. One important thing remained to be done; find the *sannyasis* and say goodbye. It took us some time to find their *ashram* among the many in Hardwar. Even then we could not just ask for our friends, but first had to pay our respects to the *Mahant* or abbot. The *Mahant* felt it his duty to entertain us, and treated our visit as an official visit; taking the opportunity to lecture us on the virtues of democracy and freedom, which was obviously his subject. It was difficult to find a suitable moment to break off, but at last it came and we said goodbye to our friends publicly in front of the *Mahant* and the other members of the sect, and were quite unable to express any of the things that were really in our hearts.

We hurried to the Dak bungalow. I changed quickly into my English clothes, and we reached the station just in time to catch the night passenger-train to Delhi, and so started our journey back to the old familiar everyday life on the sultry plains of India.

PART IV
THE 1934 PILGRIMAGE

CHAPTER 6

Taking the Plunge Again

Narrow thy path, O pilgrim lone, through wilderness wide;
Rough is the way, with rock and stone; O hast thou a Guide?
    Christ is my Guide; the Son of God
    This road so steep Himself hath trod.
Hunger and thirst, O pilgrim weak, now over thee brood;
Where, in the desert bare and bleak, obtainest thou food?
    Christ is my food; He doth impart
    His Life divine to my frail heart.
Weary thou art, O pilgrim faint, with troubles oppressed;
Out in the wild, O lonely saint, where findest thou rest?
    Christ is my rest; His Church my home;
    And Heaven's bright hosts to cheer me come.
Short is the day, O pilgrim frail; on cometh the night;
Then as the shadows deep prevail, where shalt thou find light?
    Christ is my Light; and Christ the Way
    That leads through death to endless day.

                          (Timothy Rees)

AFTER FURLOUGH IN ENGLAND I returned alone in the autumn of 1932. I went to live in Nagpur, having been lent on a half-time basis for two years to the Church of Scotland Mission. The other half of my time was given to the work of the Friends Service Council.

I was not entitled to a holiday in the hot weather of 1933 and stayed on in Nagpur. Fortunately it was the coolest hot season I can remember; the temperature never went above 104°F. Showers fell every two or three days and in shady places there was actually green grass throughout the season.

In June I abandoned the bungalow in the Civil Station provided by the Mission and went to live in the city, near the government hospital at Hansapuri, where I stayed till I left Nagpur.

My thoughts naturally turned to plans for my next hot weather holiday, and as my wife was unable to join me it was inevitable that my mind should turn again to pilgrimage. If it had been difficult in 1930 to convince myself that it was right to go, it was even more difficult in 1934. The pain in my hip that had hindered me in 1930, had considerably increased, and I had developed a noticeable limp. I knew this would be my last chance to undertake such a lengthy and arduous journey.

Khushilal also had to be considered. Although a few years younger than I, he seemed to have aged more in the last four years; but he was keen to go and his wife willing to let him. I decided to take the plunge and in every spare moment began to prepare for what I expected to be my last pilgrimage.

I had kept in correspondence with Swami Bisshuddhanand (Swami B.) and Mahadeo Banerjee, and suggested they might accompany me. Swami B. said he would not be able to go, but thought he might be in Hardwar when I passed through. Mahadeo Banerjee seriously considered the possibility and as good as promised to try and come. Swami Ram Sarikh Singh (RSS) also confirmed he intended to be in Badrinath again and would be delighted to see us there.

So in March I wrote to the Deputy Commissioner for permission to cross the 'inner line' and to the Executive Engineer at Pauri, requesting a permit to occupy the PWD rest-houses. In due course I received a letter from the Deputy Commissioner, Capt. R.H.G. Johnston, ICS. The required permit would be issued for a fee of eight *annas*, and a formal statement in writing that I would not attempt to enter Tibet. There was no response from the Executive Engineer.

In preparing for another pilgrimage I had to give my dress a great deal of thought. Since 1923 I had been using *sannyasi* costume on pilgrimage, on journeys in Bhopal State, and other visits to sacred places. In 1930, when travelling with Hindu *sannyasis*, I began to have grave doubts that it was the right thing to wear. I realised it landed me in difficulties connected with customs observed by *sadhus*, which I did not feel easy to observe myself.

Swami B. had told me that the normal greeting 'Namo Narayan', with its similar reply 'Namo Narayan' was not the equivalent of saying 'Good morning', or possibly 'worship God' as one *sannyasi* told me, but should be interpreted as 'I worship you as I worship the deity'. If this was what was in the mind of a *sadhu* who said it to me seeing my saffron clothes, I could not honestly accept that greeting, or say the same thing to him in reply. The more I came to know the customs and points of etiquette current among the *sadhus*, the more uncomfortable I became. It was true that while wearing *sannyasi* costume I had been welcomed in many places where I might not have entered wearing European clothes, and I wondered if the same results might be accomplished by wearing ordinary lay Hindu dress. The advantage of saffron-coloured clothes is they do not show the dirt so quickly and I found many laymen, whom I took for *sadhus*, wore these clothes to save themselves the trouble of washing them too often. I finally came to the decision to wear the ordinary *dhoti* and a white *kurta* (a garment like a night-shirt with long sleeves). A *kurta* could be made sufficiently roomy to put on a sweater or two underneath for warmth at higher altitudes. At lower altitudes I decided to wear my ordinary open-necked, short-sleeved cotton shirts. The *dhoti*, with English cut shirt worn outside, was common dress among students and is comfortable and cool. The costume was completed with a white *turban*.

I had taken over charge of the Friends Mission Boys' Hostel, Hoshangabad, and as Treasurer of the Friends Mission from my colleague R.D. Priestman, who had left on furlough in April, so I needed to spend a few days in Itarsi and Hoshangabad before starting on the pilgrimage. It was a hectic time with many last-minute problems to sort out, letters to write, and trying to leave everything in order in case the unexpected happened. All this with the midday temperature about 114°F in the shade and rivulets of perspiration running over skin smarting from prickly heat. I wrote on the morning of my departure to my wife: 'I am in that horrible state of mental disturbance which I usually get into before starting on a long journey or a big undertaking. By working late at night and being at work early in the morning, I think I have done all the really necessary things. If it were not for the fact that there is a mistake of Rs.55 in my cash I could go off satisfied that everything was up to date. I am sure it is only a clerical error, as I have not yet grasped R.D.P's system, but I will have to leave it, and hope I shall spot the mistake when I return'. It was not a pleasant thought that unless I found the mistake on my return in six weeks, I should have to make up the shortfall myself, when my finances would be at their lowest ebb.

Another unsettling thing was that the *mochi*, Har Lal in Itarsi, had failed me over a new pair of shoes, and I had had to get him to make another pair, which he had promised to send on the train, but they had not arrived.

In spite of further interruptions I managed to get a siesta from 12 to 1 p.m. and after two cups of tea, I was at the station in time to have my luggage weighed and booked for the train at 2.30 p.m. Before leaving I weighed myself on the station scales. On both previous occasions I had come back thinner than when I left, but had no idea of the actual weight loss. I weighed 11 stone 2½ lbs. My luggage weighed 132 lbs and Khushilal's 46 lbs.

Khushilal was already on the train and to my great relief had brought the shoes. I hurriedly tried them on and they seemed a better fit, so I discarded the first pair. Experience has taught me that footwear is most important on a pilgrimage. If your feet are comfortable you can endure many other hardships; if not, the pilgrimage can become a misery. As will be seen later, this pilgrimage was to prove by a long way the worst of any in that respect.

Beside my assorted luggage I had four large water-melons, as big as footballs, to slake our thirst on the long journey. By the time we came to eat them we had made friends with our fellow travellers in the 16-seater compartment, and the melons were much appreciated. Several had left the train by night-time and Khushilal and I were able to stretch out on the hard benches, though I had to get up several times to shake the cinders off my bedding. At Delhi we had an hour's wait and were joined by a Sikh, a fine handsome man, obviously a soldier, and two Punjabis, one a soldier, the other a sailor, who had landed in Bombay only the previous day. He had been to several English ports and enjoyed trying to keep a conversation going in English, and insisted on treating me to a cup of tea. We had to part company at Saharanpur. We shook hands all round and left the last melon with the sailor; they all seemed sorry to say goodbye.

We got a train immediately to take us to Lhaksar, the next change, so there was no time to buy any food, and nothing to be bought at any intermediate station till we got to Roorkee. There we bought some *puris*, but my enjoyment of them was spoilt by two men who got into our carriage and insisted on watching me and making remarks about me. So when one started a conversation with Khushilal I did not join in. We were soon at Lhaksar, where we all changed.

While waiting for the Dehra Dun train that was to take us to Hardwar, I had a shave by a Mohammedan barber on the platform. I never enjoy being shaved, even in a nice clean barber-shop in England, so I shall not describe my feelings on this occasion.

At Hardwar we went straight to the Dak bungalow and engaged a room. To our joy our old friend the *khansama* was still in charge. I enquired at the post office but no letter containing the permit awaited me there, so we went on to the bazaar to buy a really good warm hill blanket for Khushilal. A really good one cost the equivalent of five shillings.

Finally we went to the Bholananda Ashram hoping to find some of our old *sannyasi* friends. The oldest member, Swami Atmananda was there and very pleased to see us. But Swami B. was not. Neither was Mahadeo Banerjee who I had hoped would be waiting to accompany us; there was no news of him. His non-arrival raised a problem for me. It was partly because he had expressed the wish to revisit Kedarnath and Badrinath that I had decided to do the same pilgrimage again. But I had had a great desire to visit Gangotri, the source of the Bhagirathi river, so adding to my knowledge of the sacred places. I knew the Gangotri pilgrimage was even more arduous than the others. Most of it lies in the native state of Tehri, not in British territory. The *chattis* are fewer and further apart, and not so well organised, with no attempt to control sanitation, and poorer medical facilities. Neither Khushilal nor myself was in good enough health to take extra risks; besides our friend RSS was looking forward to our visit to Badrinath. There were still several days till I had to make a final decision.

That evening walking in Hardwar we met a handcart being hurriedly wheeled out of a *dharmshala* by the river. Covered only with a white cloth the body was in danger of being precipitated into the gutter. On enquiring we were told it was a pilgrim who had just died of cholera, and they were taking him to the burning *ghat* outside the town. Cholera is endemic most of the year in India's sacred places, and sometimes develops into an epidemic, but is usually kept more or less under control. Hardwar has a good piped water supply, safe to drink unboiled, and sanitary inspectors do their best to keep the place healthy.

New Acquaintances

At seven o'clock the next morning we made our way to the motor stand. Motor lorries now run frequently and there is plenty of competition. At Rishikesh we got another lorry to Moni ki Reti where the pilgrim's luggage is weighed at the *coolie* agency. The man in charge recognised us and was anxious to do his best for us. I had been considering trying to choose my own *coolies*, but in the end decided not to interfere with whatever might be in store for me, as I have found things go better when I keep my hands off. So we waited with interest to see what sort of companions the agent would pick for us. He produced two men almost immediately; father and son, ensuring he thought, their working well together. The father, Raju, was no beauty, but had a cheerful expression, unlike the son, who was not attractive and had a discontented expression. Having executed the contract for the journey and paid the requisite instalment in advance, we loaded up, lifted our own bundles and proceeded a short distance to our now familiar spot beside the Ganges where we slept our first night in 1923. This time I successfully ate my breakfast without being robbed by monkeys; proof that I really was an experienced pilgrim.

While we were having breakfast the *coolies* kept discreetly out of sight. When we got up to start we noticed two men with our luggage get up and follow us at a little distance. While we were in the Library at Lachhman Jhula, enquiring after the old *munshi* who had been friendly on our previous visits, the men passed us, and on overtaking them, we discovered to our astonishment, that the discontented son had been replaced by a slip of a boy who looked as if he would never stand the strain of the pilgrimage.

I demanded an explanation and Raju admitted he had played a trick on me. He had come with two sons hoping they would all get work together, but the younger one was so small, that if left behind by himself he would not get engaged. So he had swopped them, as the older had a better chance of getting work on his own. I was annoyed, as the youth was so slight, and my conscience would continually trouble me, making him carry 80 lbs of luggage over

400 miles. Raju assured me he was equal to the task and he himself would see he did not suffer. In fact, the boy, Narayan Singh was a better *coolie* than his father. He certainly carried his full share, while his father shirked his, and at the end of the day it was always Narayan Singh that did the fetching and carrying and little extra jobs that *coolies* undertake, and we had to take special care Raju did not take advantage of the boy.

We knew from past experience the importance of our relationship with the *coolies*. Once they knew we were reasonable people and wanted to treat them kindly and give them a fair deal, they responded and indeed were anxious to do their best for us. Many *coolies* are treated badly and taken advantage of by wealthy pilgrims, who considered them as slaves. We tried to think of them as friends who were helping us, and making our journey possible. We explained this to Raju and Narayan Singh and they understood that if they did their best for us, we should be neither ungrateful or ungenerous. We were surprised when Raju told us that Narayan Singh was 18 years old, and was already married. In fact the wedding had run Raju into a Rs.500 debt, and he was anxious to pay off some of this from the pilgrimage. The government fixed rate that year for the pilgrimage was the lowest I had ever paid, being Rs.50 for each *coolie* for the round trip, instead of Rs.65 in 1930, and Rs.75 in 1923. By the time we had sorted all this out I had a splitting headache as I had left without having my early morning tea.

On previous journeys I had become used to tying the *sadhu's* nether garment securely, but was not yet equally proficient in tying the *dhoti* in the style I intended to adopt for this pilgrimage. Following Khushilal's demonstration that first morning, I hoped that my *dhoti* was secure for the rest of the day, so it was unpleasant to feel it working loose and in imminent danger of descending round my ankles. There was nowhere I could retire to readjust it, so I had to grasp a handful of *dhoti* in front and try and hold myself together. In this precarious state I had to walk the whole 150 yards of the suspension bridge and on beyond the houses before I could find a place to tie myself up again.

Another disaster of that first day's march came with my footwear. Har Lal's crêpe-soled canvas shoes were good and thick and felt springy and soft on the rough road, but after a few miles had rubbed the skin away under my ankle; also a blister had developed on my right big toe joint. I changed to my old original sandals that had stood the test of the two previous pilgrimages, but before we stopped for the night the straps had punctured me in two more places.

The first night is usually a lively one. The pilgrims refreshed after their evening meal are excited by the doings of the day and all want to talk at once. A party of Punjabi women began singing with great vigour and a talkative *sadhu* wanted to impress us with stories of Krishna and Rama. Hopes of settling down early were in vain, when something like a shadow caught my eye moving on my *khariya*. I called to Khushilal to flash the torch which exposed a big scorpion. The old *sadhu* kept up his stories and presently I dozed. When I awoke he was still talking; now he was describing the Gangotri pilgrimage stage by stage in minute detail. I was just on the point of asking him to stop to let us get some sleep, when he stopped, and after a fit of coughing relapsed into silence.

Next I awoke to hear heavy rain, which soon penetrated the thatched roof and began to drip on my bedding. I shifted to a drier spot but the drips followed me. By 4 a.m. most of the pilgrims were awake and preparing to start; with further sleep out of the question, we got up and got going too.

It always seems rather a pity to miss part of the road by starting before it is light, especially if it's wooded and picturesque. We could hear the rumble of distant thunder and the sky was overcast. Soon it began to rain, lightly at first, then getting heavy. Presently hailstones the size of peas began to fall. Stones of varying sizes came rolling through the bushes and trees of the hillside above us. A lump the size of my head bounced on the path close to my feet; I never heard it coming, the thunder, wind and rain were making such a noise. I tried to protect my cameras, but my cheap umbrella from the bazaar was not waterproof, the rain coming through in a fine spray. Before long my *turban* was soaked, my *dhoti* too, and not being used to wearing one in the rain, it had not occurred to me to tuck it up in the approved manner, so it clung round my legs and made walking difficult. We were all thoroughly soaked before the storm abated.

We pressed on to Upper Bijni, hoping the caretaker of the PWD rest-house, where we had stayed before, would allow us to use it.

Rock-cut gallery near Bandarbhel *This small boy agreed to carry my*
chatti, *Khushilal and Jit Singh.* *Khariya for 1 mile for 1 anna.*

He recognised us alright, but said without the permit he could not open it up for me. To show his sympathy for our plight, and regret for not being able to oblige us, he brought us four plantains, for which he refused payment.

The sun came out and the *chattis* were full of soaking pilgrims who took off their wet clothes, festooned them over the roofs and branches and wherever they could hang them out to dry. It felt as if we had been walking for hours and must surely be time for our midday meal; but no, it was only 8 o'clock. However, we had to wait for our things to dry, so Khushilal made preparation for cooking while I made some tea on the primus stove.

We set off at noon and soon fell in with a merchant from Calcutta, Ganpati Seth. He was carrying his own bundle of bedding, which seemed too heavy for him, and he appeared glad of our company. He continued with us after resting on the ridge after the long ascent from the Hiul valley, and after our previous experiences on the long descent I prophesied that tomorrow he would be so stiff that he would find walking very painful. He did not believe me, but next morning found it was true.

About a mile from the bottom we came across a number of quite small children all hoping to earn small sums for carrying pilgrim's bundles. One boy, so small that he had not reached the stage when public opinion considered it necessary for him to wear a loin-cloth, and dressed only in a little ragged coat, marked me out as a likely customer and offered to carry my *khariya*. It contained my cameras and was moderately heavy. I had already become tired of carrying it myself. The little fellow barely came up to my waist and I was reluctant to trust him with my precious cameras. But he insisted and I gave in. I lifted the *khariya* off my shoulder and handed it to him. He swung it across his shoulder and as one end went over, it nearly swung him off his balance. It dangled about half way down his shins, so we had to tie the shoulder part to make it short enough to allow him to walk. He bargained with me for an *anna* to the *chatti* about a mile away. When we had gone about half the way, he accosted a woman *coolie* carrying a bundle on her head and made her promise to pay him half an *anna* for carrying her bundle on his head. I paid him another *pice* for posing for his photograph, and he went away feeling his luck had been in that afternoon.

Ganpati Seth was still with us when we stopped for some milk at Mahadeo next morning and he found what he was looking for; a horseman who was prepared to accept his terms and take him all the rest of the way. Soon after we started off again we heard the clatter of hoofs, and Ganpati Seth, astride a white pony, overtook us with a cheery wave of farewell. We missed him, as he had been good company and we had enjoyed his sense of humour and fun.

We lingered in the shade of the now familiar rock-cut gallery, passing along the level shady bit that goes due north before turning a sharp corner and confronting the long steep rise up to Semal *chatti* where there is little shade and the morning sun beats down. The climb is probably not more than three miles, but this time seemed never-ending. Every now and then views opened up the valleys and a range of hills over the saddle of which the footpath from Pauri comes down a side valley to Byasghat. I looked for the enormous tree, an Indian fig of some sort that had stood on the saddle which we had passed when we travelled that path in 1923, and enabled me to identify the exact spot. To my dismay it had disappeared and I felt the loss of a friend. When talking later to the local policeman and the *patwari*, I asked about the tree missing from the ridge. None of them knew anything about it. But my asking caused great interest, and they spoke as if they thought I was some government inspector who had discovered the loss of a valuable piece of government property, and someone would probably be made to account for it.

I spent the midday rest writing a long letter to my wife describing the trials I was undergoing with my sore feet. To add to the first day's blisters and sores, I had developed a big blister under the ball of my right foot, which had burst. I unwisely decided to press on instead of giving my feet a rest, as I was hobbling along in considerable pain. The *coolies* too had had enough, so lagged behind and I began to think they would never catch up. In spite of all our difficulties we had covered 16 miles during the day.

Blisters and Boils Impede the Pilgrim's Progress

One of my unremitting daily tasks was to find and boil enough water for drinking the next day. Something always seemed to happen to make this difficult and I often longed for a mighty drink of really cold water. The only cold water available, that of the Ganges, whatever the Hindus may claim, is not safe to drink unboiled, and once boiled it is a long wait for it to cool down enough to drink, and then at best is lukewarm. If the *coolies* are tired and lag behind with the primus stove, or a gusty wind is blowing, or the piped water supply at the *chatti* is hot in the pipe or insufficient, I have to resort to making tea and end up scalding my mouth in my haste. Even after four cups my thirst is not fully quenched. When it is a cold drink you want no amount of tea satisfies the longing.

My burst blister had been giving me a lot of trouble. It kept sticking to the shoe, and by trying to save it, I had developed painful calves and tender places elsewhere. On top of that, when opening a tin can I had cut my thumb on a jagged bit. I had sucked it and it soon stopped bleeding. Instead of quickly healing it had gone septic. Khushilal also seemed unwell, though he did not complain of anything specific and I put it down to increasing old age as we were both more tired than usual after a fairly easy stretch.

All morning the pain in my thumb got worse and started to throb. Rolling up my sleeve I found a clear red line running up to my armpit. We were due to spend the night at Devaprayag and I needed to look respectable, so I made an early start while the other pilgrims were waiting for the sun to go a little lower. After about half a mile I found a secluded shady place and started to change my *dhoti*. I still had not mastered the operation and remembering the near disaster at Lachhman Jhula, reinforced the fastening with safety pins.

Having made myself respectable I hurried on to Devaprayag. The post office was back in its original place by the side of the pilgrim road where it had been in 1923. Again no letter from the District Engineer about the bungalows. The postmaster thought I might have been writing to the wrong place and suggested I send a reply paid telegram to the District Engineer in Pauri.

After a short while Khushilal and the *coolies* arrived and we tried to find somewhere to stay. We had no permit for the bungalow or for the Kalikamliwala's *dharmshala,* and there are no *chattis* as pilgrims stay with their *pandas*. The postmaster promised if we could not find anything suitable he would arrange with the school-master for us to stay in the schoolhouse, which would be empty at night. After a search Khushilal found a small house we could rent. It was near the water pipe and fairly private, and we had it to ourselves. The first thing I did was boil some water and soak my throbbing thumb in a very strong solution of potassium perman-ganate. I soaked it till the skin was quite black and was relieved to find the pain decreasing. By repeated fomentation at intervals for the rest of the day the red line up my arm gradually faded.

Raju, the *coolie,* told me he was suffering from dysentery, though not severely. I gave him a tablet which acted so quickly that either he did not have dysentery or it was an interesting case of faith heal-ing; faith in the medicine.

Misfortunes never come singly. The next disaster was to dis-cover that a sore place on my foot that I thought had healed had broken down and gone septic. I began to wonder if my feet were ever going to be comfortable. To get away from the troublesome flies I went for a stroll and discovered a spring which was bricked in so could not be contaminated. It was not really cold, but I could drink as much as I wanted unboiled.

I was so tired next morning that I could hardly be bothered to get up, but forced myself to make some tea for Khushilal and myself. As the house had no sanitary arrangements I had to go for a walk. I had not realised that *panda's* agents lie in wait for early departing pilgrims, and they were dotted all along the sides of the road. They wanted to know where I was going, and the only answer I could give was that I was going to 'eat air', meaning I was going for a walk for exercise. Eventually I had to turn back and try some other direction. The walk helped to revive me and by the time I returned the initial stiffness was beginning to wear off. But later after visiting the bazaar and walking along the rocky promontory to look down at the pilgrims bathing at the confluence, I felt so lethargic that I decided to return to our room. I was not surprised to find I had a temperature which accounted for my lethargy. This left me in no doubt that I must abandon the idea of going to Gangotri.

I was not feeling much better when we left in the afternoon. No reply to my telegram had come from the District Engineer, and it felt as if a storm was about to break, but I realised the darkness was due to dust in the air, and that there must have been a dust storm on the plains. We had gone about two miles when we heard shouting behind us. It was the telegraph boy bringing the welcome news that I was allowed to use the rest-houses.

We had been given leave to use the Mission rest-house at Srinagar, so I decided to have a 'day of rest' there. The *coolies* hate hanging around, but I am sure it does pay to observe a sabbath. My feet badly needed a rest and after bathing them I put vaseline on the sore bits to stop the socks from sticking. Cheap cotton socks were available all along the route and make good bandages. By next morning my swollen feet were almost normal again.

I discovered at Srinagar that in spite of having made a careful list of all the things I needed to bring, I had left my developing tank behind. This was serious as I like to develop my films as I go along to check on the exposure. I was not hopeful of finding a replacement in the bazaar, but the unexpected happened and I found the very thing I wanted; a sort of milk can, aluminium, exactly the right size complete with lid.

Khushilal Falls Ill

We left Srinagar in the early afternoon planning to spend the night at Bhattisera where we knew from previous experience we would be comfortable. The *chatti* keeper recognised us and did everything he could to help us, allowing us to camp out in the open air among the terraced tobacco fields behind the *chatti*, where the irrigation channels provide water for cooking and washing. The *coolies* were late in arriving having taken five hours to do the eight miles. After dark the fireflies performed brilliantly for our benefit as they danced among the tobacco plants.

We were up and ready to tackle the steep climb to Chhantikhal ridge before dawn. Some men we overtook were laughing at a poor village pilgrim who was carrying a heavy load of sacred Ganges sand he had picked up at Lachhman Jhula, and intended to carry for the 400 miles of the pilgrimage and distribute as *prasad* among his relatives when he got home.

At Khankra the *coolies* said they did not want to go beyond the next *chatti*. Two long ascents during one morning were enough, they said. As I had not made tea for myself before starting I had developed a severe headache. By the time I was able to make myself some tea it was almost too late and I had to lie down, but the tea did its job and we had our breakfast early. No sooner had we finished than the rain came on. We waited in the hopes of it stopping. We were aiming for Rudraprayag where I hoped to occupy the bungalow. When we reached it we found the District Engineer was expected that day, so we went along to the school, and the headmaster made us very welcome and gave us permission to stay the night.

I discovered that one of the reasons why the *coolies* were so slow was that Raju had developed boils on his back. I hated having to use a *coolie* in that condition, but he did not want to give up as he would lose his money. Neither Khushilal nor I felt able to carry anything more ourselves, so though it seemed cruel we had to allow Raju to reduce his load by giving whatever he could to Narayan Singh.

Early the following morning I boiled water for tea and to foment Raju's boils. Then I went to call on the District Engineer. He told me the Deputy Commissioner, Captain Johnston, new to the district, was following the pilgrimage and was ahead of me. Before setting off I boiled more water and fomented Raju's back. Then once again I went too far before stopping for the blisters that were trying to heal. But we had an agreeable surprise; the next *chatti* was an ideal one. I found the best bathing pool anywhere on the pilgrimage, and all the discomforts, and even the blisters, seemed to fade into insignificance.

Every morning now I boiled water to make tea as well as foment Raju's back, which delayed our starting, but the tea was essential to prevent splitting headaches later.

What with my feet and Raju's back I had not been keeping an eye on Khushilal properly, till one midday break when I noticed he did not eat anything. He walked very slowly all afternoon, lagging behind, instead of going on in front as usual. At Bheri I was almost immediately 'discovered' by an English-speaking young man. I was amazed by his fluency, accuracy and pronunciation and felt ashamed that after 23 years in India, my Hindi was no better than it was. He insisted on my going to his house where he said his mother would prepare tea for me. At last it arrived along with a juicy hot *paratha*. I ate it as quickly as possible as I was anxious to get back to Khushilal. We exchanged names and addresses and I discovered he was a Mohammedan. I was thankful that the questions he had asked me about Islam I had answered in such a way that they could not have given any offence.

I found that Khushilal had finished cooking and was lying down and assumed he had eaten what he wanted. He seemed too tired to talk, other than to apologise for the *chapatis* which were not up to his usual standard.

Looking back I wondered if I should have realised earlier that there was something wrong with Khushilal. In the morning I asked him how he was, but he did not complain of any special trouble. We had more than five miles to go that morning; the last three a stiff climb exposed to the full glare of the morning sun. Half way up the climb, I took the opportunity to continue a letter to my wife and wrote: 'I am on the road, having gained enormously on Khushilal on the long steep ascent. It's a gorgeous spot, high up on the mountainside, under a kind of weeping willow that gives thick shade. The view in front is magnificent. If only I were an artist I would try and draw it. The Kedarnath range is peeping down two valleys divided by a succession of lower hills rising one above the other. To the right Chaukhamba is visible. I cannot make out what is wrong with Khushilal; no fever, and nothing that might prevent him walking, but up this long steep bit into Guptkashi, I soon outstripped him'.

While I was on the hill I was overtaken by a man riding on a white pony who handed me two postal communications; a letter from a friend on the plains, and the other a single sheet supplement of the local Nagpur newspaper, the *Hitaveda*, giving the matriculation results for the Central Provinces. Who the man was, and how he got hold of them, I never found out. As I was at the time in charge of the Hislop Collegiate High School (Church of Scotland Mission) in Nagpur, I was particularly interested in the Matric results, so I sat down and went through them, and was pleased to find that some of our own boys from Hoshangabad had also been successful.

After Khushilal caught me up at the weeping willow, we went on together, and just outside Guptkashi he began to retch violently. He admitted he had been sick in the night and had not eaten anything last night.

We were given a small room to ourselves in the Kalikamliwala's *dharmshala* at Guptkashi. The floor was covered with a *ringal* strip mat, and Khushilal lay down in the corner and covered himself up completely. Now that I knew Khushilal was really ill I had to decide what I was going to do.

There was no dispensary at Guptkashi but there was a government hospital at Ukhimath, exactly opposite and at the same height on the other side of the valley. A bare two miles as the crow flies, but a good half day's march down some thousands of feet to the river and then up the other side, for mere human beings.

I recalled what had happened in 1923 when Khushilal was ill and again in 1930, when he had been cured in answer to prayer, and I felt confident that when evening came, we could pray together and he would be alright again. I thought the best place to stay that night would be Bhenta, where the pilgrims leave their surplus luggage on the way up to Kedarnath. It was only two miles further on and Khushilal said he would follow when he felt able. When he arrived, as it looked likely to be a fine night, I decided it would be pleasanter to sleep out of doors. I had earlier discovered a suitable spot, a few yards back from the road, a bathing tank with running water from two stone spouts, and with a stone pavement surround. So we settled down there. Again Khushilal ate practically nothing, but lay down and tried to sleep, while I waited till evening.

It was quiet and peaceful under a clear starry sky and we were left undisturbed. I knelt by Khushilal and prayed that he might be healed.

Alone to Kedarnath

In the morning Khushilal was no better so I decided to take him to Ukhimath hospital. I found a stalwart *coolie* with a *kandi* willing and able to carry Khushilal on his back to Ukhimath. There was a new doctor at the hospital, Dr Chintamani Anthwal, who welcomed us and was interested that we had stayed at the hospital twice before. This time the operating theatre was empty and he admitted Khushilal as an in-patient there, as it was larger and more airy than any in-patient room.

Dr Anthwal examined Khushilal thoroughly and assured me that it was not too serious and he would soon put him right. By the evening with Khushilal's consent I decided to push on to Kedarnath alone. He knew how anxious I was to get that photograph of the

The spring near Bhenta where Khushilal lay ill in 1934.

temple that I had missed the last time. We agreed that Narayan Singh would come with me, and Raju would stay with Khushilal, enabling him to have a rest and get his boils treated.

It was a new experience setting out on my own. In Ukhimath I had heard that the Deputy Commissioner, Captain Johnston, and his wife were already up in Kedarnath. The possibility of meeting an English lady and the chief official of the district, made me consider what clothes I had that were suitable for such an occasion. I had one clean shirt left, a light blue poplin with short sleeves; not really suitable at an altitude of 12,000 feet. The alternative was to put on one of my *kurtas* so that I could wear a sweater underneath and keep warm.

I told Khushilal I would not be away more than six days. Two days each way for walking, the distance being 26 miles, and two days at Kedarnath, hoping for at least one fine clear morning when I could take photographs.

Narayan Singh had only a light load and no father to keep making him sit down for a smoke, so we were able to travel faster than we had been doing for many days. We did eight miles before breakfast, another six in the afternoon; 14 miles with several steep climbs would have been good enough for one day. But if I could make Gaurikund, another five miles, it would leave only the last seven-mile-long climb up to Kedarnath, which I should be able to do before breakfast the next morning. So I pushed on without thinking of the weather. The sky became overcast and a strong wind got up. I waited for Narayan Singh and took my umbrella from his load. There was no shelter for four miles, mostly uphill and it seemed never to end. The rain came on and made the paths slippery and I reached Gaurikund tired and wet long after dark.

I did not have a restful night having left the Keatings powder behind to lighten the load, and felt stiff and unrefreshed the next morning. The final climb begins immediately and my *khariya* with my cameras and other necessities seemed to weigh a ton. While I was resting at a *chatti* where hot milk was available, a *coolie* with an empty *kandi* passed and I asked if he would carry my bundle. He said he would for a *rupee*. Two days' pay for two hours' work. I offered him eight *annas*; he refused, so I took up my burden and slowly started off again.

My strength ran out with three miles to go. I could not understand why I felt so feeble. Here of all places where I had carried
the old Punjabi lady up the hill only four years ago, and now I
was scarcely able to drag myself along. While I was resting, some
pilgrims I knew passed, and seeing my state took my *khariya* and
gave it to their *gumastar* (*panda's* agent), who slung it over his shoulders. I realised I was suffering from mountain sickness, and felt as
if I was going to be violently sick and yet could not bring myself to
let it come. Those last three miles were a long drawn out agony.
With hindsight I was thankful for the experience, as I learned what
many weaker and less nourished pilgrims endure, and know from
experience now what many others suffer.

By the time I reached the place from where the temple and
town of Kedarnath can be seen, the morning sun had disappeared
and clouds covered the peaks. I was in my clean light blue short-
sleeved shirt. The wind blew colder, heavy clouds formed behind
me and down came the hail, large enough stones to sting. The hail
turned to sleet and I was miserably cold. I tried to quicken my pace.
At last I reached the bridge over the river with the last steep ascent
into the town. A *panda* recognised me, and seeing me shivering
took off his own overcoat and wrapped it round my shoulders.
Several others came to my aid and took me to the Kalikamliwala's
dharmshala. They gave me a small room and brought blankets as
Narayan Singh had not yet arrived. Then they brought me some
sweet tea, flavoured with cloves, cinnamon and cardamon seeds
and did all they could to make me comfortable. I had no idea that
what was really the matter was that my temperature had gone up.

The Deputy Commissioner had found camping impossible and
had moved into a good house belonging to the leading family of
pandas. I gave one of the *pandas* my visiting card and asked him to
give it to the Commissioner and tell him where I was and what was
the matter.

To my surprise at 4 o'clock, a *chaprasi* in uniform, belt and
brass badge, called and said in the customary Hindu idiom, 'The
Sahib is calling you'. I had no desire to move from the warmth of
my blankets. I had not shaved, my shirt was no longer fresh having
been soaked in the rain. All I could do was put a sweater on over
my shirt, which emphasised the bulge caused by the tying of my

Kedarnath 1934.

dhoti, but I had reached the point of not caring what sort of impression I created, and nothing could be done to redeem the situation.

The *chaprasi* led me to the house and as I approached I saw a small child, and I realised that I was not only going to meet the Deputy Commissioner in my present unsightly condition, but also his wife. Suddenly a lady wearing jodhpur breeches came out of the house and in spite of the shock she must have got showed no sign of it, and gave me a most warm welcome. Captain Johnston arrived and we all went inside where tea was produced. They asked me back for dinner, which they had fairly early, and after that I returned to the *dharmshala* and had a good night's rest.

The next morning I felt much better. It was gloriously fine, the peaks clear of cloud and the light brilliant. Captain Johnston was out soon after me, and we both became busy with our cameras. This was what I had longed for; the view of the temple that I had wanted so badly. I took six exposures from different places. There was an interesting group of *sadhus*, sitting in a circle round a glowing log fire. They had been out all night in spite of the sharp frost, none the worse for the experience as *sadhus* inure themselves to complete indifference to extreme heat or cold.

Several men below the steps had baskets of flowers for sale to the pilgrims for offerings inside the temple. There was a profusion of wild flowers all over the mountainsides, which begin to bloom almost as soon as the snow melts. The most common at that time is a kind of mauve primula.

I had breakfast with the Johnstons after which Captain Johnston intended to go exploring. He asked me to join him, and I was tempted, as I knew I would not get another opportunity. I particularly wanted to see Brahmagupha, where the Pandava brothers are said to have performed the Yagnya ceremony, and where Shankaracharya is said to have died; and Bhaironjhamp, the cliff from which *sadhus* used to commit suicide. I had stood on top of a similar Bhaironjhamp near the sacred cave at Amarnath in Kashmir, and would have liked to identify it properly this time, but thought I had better not risk it.

During the morning Mrs Johnston kindly arranged for me to have a hot bath. This consisted of two inches of hot water, heated in blackened oil tins poured into a galvanised bath, part of the Deputy Commissioner's travelling outfit. To me it was a great luxury and remembered with much gratitude. Soon after I began to shiver as my temperature was up again, and I was thankful I had not gone exploring. The Johnstons sent a message when dinner was ready, but I thought I had better stay where I was and not eat anything. Later Mrs Johnston sent a *chaprasi* with a hot-water bottle which was just what I needed and I had quite a good night.

The Johnstons were planning to leave the next morning and I was up and ready to start before them. They sent a message for me to wait and have breakfast with them; which delayed my start but was a much better breakfast than anything I could have got at Gaurikund. They overtook me as I was talking to a *sadhu* coming up the hill who remembered me from the Amarnath pilgrimage, and was very pleased to see me again. At Gaurikund the Johnstons invited me to share their picnic lunch of tongue turnovers and cold vegetables. In spite of my beard and bulge the Johnstons could not have been kinder.

Although I was well within the time limit I had set myself, I was anxious to get back to Khushilal, so though it was Sunday I walked another seven miles, leaving only 12 for the next day. On Monday morning Narayan Singh said he had heard from someone coming up that Khushilal was alright again. By 11.30 I had covered nine miles and reached the place where the road divides and took the left fork down the steep descent to the bridge over the

Mandakini to the equally steep ascent to Ukhimath. The heat was tremendous with the sun directly overhead; it just shrivels you up, especially at the end of a long morning's march.

Rounding a bend I had the first view of the hospital and could make out a little spot of saffron colour on the verandah. I put my fingers in my mouth and let out my best whistle, but Khushilal was not expecting me so early, and I did not succeed in making him look up.

When I stepped onto the verandah he was delighted to see me back. He was better but still very weak. He had only just been able to eat a small *chapati* and some lentils. He admitted that he had almost given up hope of seeing me again. Dr Anthwal had waited on him personally and could not have been kinder or more thoughtful. We both had a lot to be thankful for.

Sunrise on Tungnath

Khushilal was obviously not fit to start out again the next day. I also needed time to clean myself up, do some writing and develop my photographs. After a rest and a cup of tea I tackled my photographs using the convenient little spring nearby for washing them. Khushilal kindly washed my *turban* and shirt and spread them out in the sun to dry. Dr Anthwal wanted me to photograph his only son, a small babe, with his pet rabbit. Then he added a small nephew and two other children. As I was getting this organised, the sound of drums on the hillside made me aware that Captain Johnston must be approaching the town. I did not want to miss the town's welcome to the Deputy Commissioner, so as the clean shirt

The sacred spring in Ukhimath hospital compound, where we stayed on all three pilgrimages, and Khushilal was a patient for 10 days in 1934.

and *turban* were still wet, I had to go as I was, accompanied by Dr Anthwal, and reached the road just in time to see the procession. It was led by Sher Singh, the manager of the temple, followed by a band of many weird instruments and a choir of school boys. They swept up the steep path, carrying the Deputy Commissioner along as on the crest of a wave. The doctor and I fell in with them to the bazaar, when I had had enough. The strains of the band died away as the procession went on through the town to the tents pitched for the Deputy Commissioner further up the hill.

I wondered what had happened to Mrs Johnston and found her struggling along on her own. She was greatly relieved to see me and I accompanied her through the bazaar until we met Sher Singh coming down the hill, and he took charge. Mrs Johnston kindly invited me up later for a meal at the camp.

I then returned to the doctor's house to collect the children and the white rabbit. I had one exposure left and to my dismay a dog was now produced to add to the group. When I developed the photograph, to my amazement, rabbit, dog and all four children were clearly recognisable.

By then my clean shirt and *turban* were nearly dry. Khushilal tied the *turban* in the truculent Punjabi style he thinks suits me better than when I tie it myself, when according to him I look like an unemployed *khidmatgar* (table waiter). Dressed and properly shaved, I felt I had achieved what I had aimed at when I planned to introduce myself to the Johnstons at Kedarnath. I hurried up the hill. Their belongings had not arrived, but their English mail had, and they offered me the *Illustrated London News* which was a great treat for me and kept me happy till the food arrived.

Next morning Khushilal was feeling much better so we were off soon after 6 a.m. Taking it easy on the climbs it took us four hours to do six miles. Much to my relief Khushilal stood up to it well, and was able to cook some *khichari* for us both at midday. We were now passing through one of the most beautiful parts of the whole pilgrimage, so it was a pleasure to linger among the giant forest trees, and we seemed to have it to ourselves.

After a good night at the well-positioned PWD bungalow Khushilal felt able to tackle the climb to Tungnath. Since our 1930 visit the six-foot-wide road had been completed right up to the temple, making our climb very much easier. There were only a few

Chaukhamba from near the summit of Tungnath.

pilgrims bathing and drying their clothes near the tank, and it was easy to find a quiet room to ourselves in the Kalikamliwalas' *dharmshala*. We chose an upper room from which I could watch the *pandas* and the pilgrims outside. We had fun with an old lady who asked Khushilal for '*chaya*'. Khushilal could not believe she meant what he thought she did. So she made herself perfectly clear by saying 'tea', whereupon he passed her on to me and we had a good laugh trying to understand each other. We had no problem when she came back asking for *chini*.

I spent most of the afternoon roaming about the temple precincts with my camera. Quite by accident I stumbled on one of the most interesting things I had seen. Eight *pandas*, or people connected with the temple, a *sadhu* and four children, were sitting in a circle on the flagged platform in front of the temple, eating the *bhog*, the sacred food that had been offered at the temple, piled high on their brass plates. I thought of the early Christians in the church at Corinth, writing to Paul to ask his advice on the subject of food offered to idols, and I was reminded that a Christian must act from love as well as knowledge. They were enjoying their meal and had no objection to my taking photographs.

Most pilgrims go down after the midday halt, but I wanted to stay overnight so as to be able to see the sunset and sunrise from the summit. The sunset was disappointing as the atmosphere was darkened by extensive forest fires that had been burning for several days. I was up early the following morning to be on the summit before the sunrise, and hurried panting up the rough track keeping an eye on the eastern peaks sharply outlined against the glowing sky. One by one the higher peaks were tipped with gold, before the rim of the sun appeared above the eastern peaks, then the glare made them invisible. As the red glow disappeared in the brilliance of the full sunlight, I realised that the time before the sunrise was much the more worthwhile. I was reluctant to leave as this I was sure would be my last visit. I had agreed with Khushilal where we would meet at midday only a few miles downhill; so there was no need to hurry. I was looking forward to one particular spot on the path where I had gathered wild strawberries, and sure enough when I reached it, the hillside was covered with plants and the strawberries were ripe. I gathered enough for Khushilal and myself to share for breakfast. They were not very big, but when he had eaten half a dozen at a time with concentrated Klim, Khushilal got a faint idea of what English strawberries and cream tasted like.

While I was carrying the strawberries I was overtaken by one of the Deputy Commissioner's servants, hurrying ahead to make arrangements for his advance camp. He told me he had been at Pauri when I stayed there with the then Deputy Commissioner and his wife, Mr and Mrs Acton, in 1923, and that he remembered my visit.

Pipalkoti's Postal Grievance

At Chamoli I went along to the Post Office hoping to find several weeks' English mail collected up. There was only one lot from which I learnt that my eldest son had been ill and had had an operation, but as the previous letter was missing I had no idea what the trouble had been. I clambered down to the river to find a place to wash my feet so that I could go along to the hospital for treatment. Dr Anthwal had told us that his father was compounder at the Chamoli hospital, but I could find neither the doctor nor the compounder. I walked into one of the wards which was clean, tidy and airy; the one patient, a *sadhu* whom I recognised was glad to have someone to talk to.

I searched the bazaar without much hope, for shops that sold cheap shoes, but found a friendly Hindu who kept a general store. He found a pair of canvas shoes which I could just squeeze into, and I laid in a supply of socks which I still needed as bandages. He also had oil for the primus, sunlight soap and sultanas. Commenting on my Indian clothes he asked whether I had become their brother, and I told him I tried to look upon all as my brothers. He later intervened on my behalf when two *sadhus*, knowing I was English and assuming that I must be wealthy, started to beg very persistently, and told them to regard me as an ordinary Indian.

I waited at Chamoli till the afternoon mail-bags arrived, but there was no sign of my missing mail. I hurried off to catch up with Khushilal and the *coolies*. Half a mile out I discovered that I had forgotten to post my letter to my wife, and was tempted to return, but it would have delayed me an hour and added to my tiredness. I decided to risk posting it in the box at Chhinka which is opened up by a shopkeeper when the mail runner comes through from higher up the valley. The risk paid off as the letter arrived in due course. Next morning we passed through Hat before the steep zig-zag climb to Pipalkoti, and while I was sitting resting outside one of the shops, several shopkeepers gathered and told me of their grievances regarding the post office. Unfortunately a succession of postmasters, all Kshattriyas, had been untrustworthy and dismissed one after the other. Finally the authorities had decided to shift the post office to Hat. So now every time the traders needed the post office they had to make the journey down to Hat and back and found it a great hardship. They begged me to do something. I told them I would mention their problem to the Deputy Commissioner. Whether my intervention on their behalf had any effect I do not know.

At the time E.E. Shipton and H.W. Tilman were in the area, just two weeks ahead of me, and E.E. Shipton wrote in his book *Nanda Devi*, how they had been waiting for their porters to catch up sitting talking to the shopkeepers at Pipalkoti, and had had an identical request.

Later I found a pilgrim lying by the side of the road. He seemed to be ill, not merely sleeping, so I stopped to investigate. He was suffering from a high fever and was exhausted from thirst. Pilgrims do not consider it their business to interfere; the man is reaping the due reward of his actions in a previous birth. Nor do they carry water with them, and if they did would not offer it to a man of a different caste. I was doubtful if he would accept water from me, even to save his life, but I poured some water from my flask into my tumbler and held it to his lips. He drank until he finished every drop I had. It acted like magic, and in a few minutes he was on his feet and staggered off on his way home.

A little further on the road we had used in 1930 had disappeared in a very big landslide. The climb to circumvent it was alarmingly steep and in places looked very insecure with nothing but a sheer drop to the river below. It seemed a desperate place for ponies and *dandi coolies* especially as it was impossible for riders to remain seated or passengers to sit in their *dandis* or *jhampans*, so all had to dismount and walk; just at the place they most needed to be carried. The wealthy and the infirm pilgrims found themselves confronted with a climb quite beyond their capabilities, and the *coolies* had to use all their ingenuity to get them up. The great advantage was that instead of a long fairly steep climb by the old road, the very steep new road came out much higher up, and we were almost then in sight of our goal, Badrinath.

Ram Sharikh Singh's Initiation

I had gone ahead of Khushilal on the stiff climb as I wanted to find the caretaker and have the bungalow opened up. Looking back from my vantage point I could see Khushilal had been joined by a stout figure in black. It crossed my mind that it might be our old friend RSS. When they came nearer I saw that it was indeed RSS, so altered that I hardly recognised him. Previously he had been clean-shaven; now he had grown a beard and his hair was long and fluffy, standing out all round his head like a halo. His dark garment was made of homespun hill cloth. He brought to mind my idea of an ancient Hebrew prophet or John the Baptist.

The warm welcome he gave us made me thankful that we had not turned back after all our discouragements and difficulties. He had heard that the Deputy Commissioner was expected and would be occupying the bungalow, so he had been trying to find other accommodation for us. But I had set my heart on staying in the bungalow and it was settled that we would stay there to start with anyway.

Although our friend's servant was ill, he invited us to come straight to his cottage for tea and Quaker oats. RSS likes to do everything exactly right and without hurry, but with due deliberation and the dignity befitting such an occasion. He brought out a tin of Quaker oats and a primus stove like mine on which to cook. There was so much to talk about that he would stop with spoon poised in mid air while he continued talking, but eventually our appetites were appeased with a steaming bowl of porridge, followed half an hour later by some tea. He was enjoying himself and we were thoroughly enjoying his company and conversation.

All that day as I had been marching I was aware of new sore places on my feet, and I was looking forward to being able to wash them in the pond behind the bungalow and have plenty of water to heat and foment them. As soon as I was free to explore I discovered the pond had disappeared, and to our dismay we found the springs had practically stopped running. It took me some time even to collect enough water for drinking. There had not been much snow up at Badrinath that year, so there was no moisture in the ground. By morning my foot had gone septic and I went along to the hospital close by and saw the doctor, under whose skill it soon began to improve.

While I was in Badrinath I made a very painful discovery about my photography. As I developed the films I noticed that most of them appeared slightly out of focus. I put it down to old age and that my hand must be getting shaky, although the first roll had been perfectly sharp and as good as any I had taken. I used a tripod to take a series of the town from our side of the river, but again every one was slightly out of focus. Something must have altered the position of the front of the camera when I pulled it out to focus it, as the foreground was sharp, but the distance blurred. It was heartbreaking to realise what was going on, as I had no hope of re-visiting and the pilgrimage was now practically over. Even the hard-earned precious photos of Kedarnath temple would never really make good enlargements or lantern slides. I only had four films left, sufficient for 32 exposures. I did my best to allow for the error, and though the results were better, they still were not perfect. To make things worse, my Vest Pocket Kodak was old and the bellows had given way while I was in Kashmir in 1929. I had had the bellows renewed, but it had never been satisfactory since. After my return I sent the camera to Kodak in Bombay, but they were unable to explain the mystery.

On the Saturday I received definite news that the Deputy Commissioner would arrive next morning, so made preparations to vacate the bungalow in good time. We were given a good-sized room to ourselves in the 'Punjabi *Kshetra*' where pilgrims from the Punjab stay, run by a charitable organisation. There was no furniture but a cotton *darri* was spread on the floor especially for us. Soon after we had settled RSS came to see us and we had tea together. He had never actually said straight out that he had become a Christian, but I had gathered that that was so. He had told Khushilal that two *sadhus* had become Christians through his teaching. On this occasion he said plainly he had had a personal experience of Christ last year which he referred to as his 'initiation'. He used both the English word and the Hindi word *diksha*, signifying the receiving of the initiatory 'mantra' from a spiritual teacher.

RSS returned in the evening, and sat with us while we had our meal. One advantage of living in the Punjabi *kshetra* was that Khushilal was saved the trouble of cooking as they provided all the pilgrims with as many *chapatis* as they needed. After we had finished I made some cocoa which RSS drank with us, before settling down to a Quaker Meeting for Worship, during which I felt led to speak of Christ's threefold legacy of Peace, Joy and Love. As had happened on previous occasions, worship again passed into speaking of those things that were nearest to our hearts.

Ram Sarikh Singh asked me to write something in the Scofield Bible I had sent him after our second meeting, and I copied out the 'Commission' that Paul received at the time of his conversion on the Damascus road (Acts XXVI, 16-18): 'I have appeared unto thee for this purpose, to make thee a minister and a witness, both of those things which thou hast seen, and of those things in which I will appear unto thee. I send thee unto the nations, to open their eyes and to turn them from darkness to light, and from the power of Satan unto God, that they may receive forgiveness of sins, and inheritance among them which are sanctified by faith which is in me.' I had always felt that when Ram Sarikh Singh became a

Christian with his knowledge of Hinduism he had the possibility of becoming an apostle to India, like Paul to the Gentiles.

On our last morning we went along to have breakfast with Ram Sarikh Singh in his cottage facing across the river to the temple. As it was Sunday we had a time of worship with him, and I felt it laid upon me to remind him of the necessity to be constant in his reading of the Bible, as he was so keen a student of Hindu and other philosophy, that he might be in danger of neglecting what was even more important. I pointed out that Christ himself must have been a careful student of the Scriptures, and if He found it necessary, and was able to gain inspiration from the Old Testament writings, it was far more vital for us to nourish our spiritual life by regular Bible study. We spoke of meditation, but I pointed out, we cannot expect God to speak to us in a miraculous way to save us the trouble of studying what He has already revealed.

While we were waiting for breakfast, I showed him what I had written in his Bible and said that I hoped and prayed that the time would come when he too would be conscious of a special commission to pass on to his countrymen the vision that he himself had received. Then I read John 14 and Ram Sarikh Singh told me he had been reading the same chapter only the day before.

After breakfast Khushilal ventured to suggest that Ram Sarikh Singh should allow me to take his photograph. I had asked him on previous visits and he had always declined, saying he did not feel worthy of it. As this was likely to be the last time we should meet him in Badrinath, Khushilal especially wished to make one more effort to persuade him. But at the very mention of the word 'photo', he disappeared inside and did not come out again. After a while we followed him in, reassured him, and let him have his way.

It is interesting that in E.E. Shipton's book *Nanda Devi*, he tells of a similar experience with Ram Sarikh Singh:

> 'But a far more interesting ascetic than the hermits of the Bhasudhara was a professor, Ram Sarikh Singh, known to all in the district as "the Master". We had met him first in Badrinath, whither he came every year, not to stay in the town but to withdraw, with a single attendant, to a tent pitched on a green alp in the shadow of the beautiful Nilkanta. There, in the midst of scenery grand and inspiring, he passed his time in reading and meditation. Deeply learned in Hindu religion and philosophy, and also in the traditions of these

mountain regions, his learning had not been gained from books alone since he was a lover of mountain travel and had journeyed extensively, even to Mount Kailas in Tibet, which lay some hundred miles to the north-east and was of the greatest sanctity to both Hindu and Tibetan. We spent many delightful hours with "the Master" in his wild and secluded valley, and the memory of them is among the fondest of our travels.... That there is no portrait of "the Master" in these pages is what we call "our fault". He, however, out of the depths of his philosophy refers to it as Providential (in the strictest meaning of that word). Before setting out to visit him at his camp we constantly reminded each other about a camera, hoping that he would permit us to photograph him – and in the end, both of us inevitably forgot it! When we told him of the omission he displayed great satisfaction, and laughingly told us that never had he had his photograph taken, and saw, in this last narrow escape, the directing hand of some Higher Power determined to protect his immunity.' (*pp. 195-7*)

Khushilal left to see to the departure of the *coolies* and the luggage, and I was left for a last talk with Ram Sarikh Singh. He had plenty to talk about, and ordered Saligram to light his huqah. He smoked and the huqah gurgled as he talked, but soon he became so interested in what he was saying that the huqah went out, and Saligram had to re-light it. At last the moment came when we must part. He told me that this visit had given him far more pleasure than either of the previous visits, and I felt it would have been well worth while our coming all that way, even if we had not met or spoken to anyone else.

Before separating we embraced each other in the Hindustani fashion, and I clambered back up the stones that had been placed for steps up the steep bank behind the cottage, and waved good-bye as I disappeared on the more level ground beyond.

First thing that morning I had re-packed everything ready for starting on the homeward journey, and changed into clean clothes so that I might call on Captain and Mrs Johnston when they arrived; probably my last opportunity of meeting them. It was a dull threatening morning, with heavy clouds low down on the hills. I went along to the hospital to have my foot dressed, and cannot speak too highly of the care and kindness of Dr P.N. Khanduri, under whose skill my feet were improving rapidly.

I received a warm welcome from the Johnstons who had arrived and settled in at the bungalow. Even the baby seemed pleased to see me again. By that time the rain had come on and the Johnstons pressed me to stay, but I had promised to catch up Khushilal as soon as I could. My umbrella did little to protect me from a soaking, and as usual I found the fear of getting wet is the worst part. Once thoroughly soaked you can enjoy anything that happens. So by the time I began the steep descent I realised the clouds were giving me a completely different and very beautiful aspect of the familiar hills. Masses of grey cloud filled the side valleys, pierced by mountains forming a series of silhouettes of steep hillsides ridged with pine trees, standing out black against the cloud. They ranged one behind the other ever higher, instead of melting one into another indistinctly as on a clear day.

The wet made the diversion over the landslide even more treacherous. My crepe rubber soles had no grip, and I skidded on several occasions, recovering myself with great difficulty. My umbrella got badly damaged and afforded no protection, and I was thankful to reach more level and wider paths above Hanuman *chatti*. I was hurrying through Hanuman *chatti*, trying to make up for the slowness on the descent, when I heard someone call, and found Khushilal and the *coolies*. With a good hour's start I had expected they were well ahead of me, and was a bit disappointed to find they had stopped after doing only five miles. Khushilal was greatly tickled by my attempts to tuck my *dhoti* up to prevent the wet cloth flapping round my legs, and begged to be allowed to photograph me, but my pride forbade it, which I now regret. A picture would have been a much more striking record of the day's experience than anything I can describe in words.

On the way up to Badrinath, we found that the suspension bridge above Lambagar had been washed away in a flood the previous year. Now as we approached it a regular traffic jam had built up. Dozens of pilgrims, *coolies* with their loads, ponies with passengers, loaded mules and their drivers were all waiting their turn to cross in both directions the temporary rope bridge, made of 18-inch-wide planks strung between the pillars of the old bridge. There were men controlling the traffic at each end, allowing small groups of four pilgrims, or one loaded pony and driver to pass at a time. The bridge swayed considerably, especially in the middle

The bridge above Lambagar chatti *was swept away in 1933, and was replaced by this suspension bridge, causing long hold-ups.*

and many were hesitant to step out on to something so insecure. We stood and watched for some time and enjoyed the excitement provided by one mule that strongly objected to making the crossing. Its protest did not take the form of violence, but of non-cooperation; just refusing to budge. So they tied a rope to one of its front legs, and two men pulled while a third pushed behind, and together they succeeded in getting the animal across.

Our aim now was to make for home as quickly as our *coolies* would let us. I had my eye on the bungalow at Pipalkoti where I hoped to develop my photographs, but found there was no water near by. So we had to go on till we found a suitable *chatti* where I could get all the water I needed. The going is now easier, and passing through Chamoli enters the stretch of valley back to Rudraprayag which we do not touch on the outward journey. From Chamoli to Nandprayag is a pleasant march mostly on the level. Nandprayag is where the firm of P. Mahesha Nand Sharma and Sons, who publish postcards from my photographs, has its headquarters. Nandprayag is a great centre for the manufacture of Shilajit, a bituminous substance extracted from rocks. Sharma and Sons claim to have the oldest established factory of Shilajit in

Nandprayag, producing the best quality product. The popularity of Shilajit seems to have increased enormously since I was first shown over Sharma and Sons factory in 1923. Shilajit is typical of huge numbers of patent medicines and drugs widely advertised in Indian newspapers, with wild claims to cure all sorts of lurid and intimate symptoms and diseases.

The last of the five great junctions is at Karnprayag. After bathing here the main stream of pilgrims leave the Ganges valley and turn south, over the hills to Ranikhet, on the railway line. I had never arrived at the right time to see the bathing, so made a special effort to reach the *sangam* while the bathing was still in progress. The *sangam* is visible more than a mile away, and I could see a small crowd of bathers. As I got nearer I could see it was going to be a race between me and a dark storm-cloud coming up the valley. By the time I reached the junction, a strong wind was blowing and drops of rain were beginning to fall. Only a few bathers were left, the rest having hurriedly collected their things and fled to escape the storm.

The larger of the two temples at the junction is above the road, and has a tall tower typical of the district. To my surprise I found the officiating priest was a graduate of Allahabad University who had passed the Intermediate examination from Ewing Christian College. The smaller temple stands in a clump of trees below the level of the road. A flight of solid stone steps leads down from the road to the river. In a commanding position at the foot sits the Brahman in charge of the Shaivite symbol, who marks the foreheads and accepts the offerings of the returning bathers. The junction is at the tip of a long tongue covered with white boulders, and the bathing the safest of all the five junctions. At the tip I found four small pine trees planted to form a square surrounded with a low wall of boulders. A few *sadhus* were finishing their bathe while the *pandas* were dismantling their 'office' before making for shelter themselves, leaving the place deserted till another crowd assembled the next day.

The afternoon march brought us to Gauchar, one of the sites selected as a landing ground for the aeroplane service to Badrinath. No regular service had started, but planes from Hardwar had landed there and by 1936 when I was in Hardwar planes were going every day to Agastmuni and Gauchar. There was still no talk of their going on to Badrinath or Kedarnath, but it seemed strange that I could return to Hardwar from Gauchar in 45 minutes, but walking would take me six days.

I set off across the landing strip in search of a bathe. It was further than I thought down to the river, and I had to clamber over rocks and under thick thorny bushes. When I got to the edge the current was too strong for a swim and I had to be content with a wash. It was getting dark as I started back and in my haste I trod heavily on a thorny branch, and a thorn went right through the thin crêpe rubber sole and deep into my toe. I could not pull the thorn out, so I had to drag my foot out of the shoe, tearing my toe in the process and then break off the point of the thorn which fortunately came away with the shoe. The toe was so sore I thought part of the thorn must have been left in, but the next day it was better and I walked eight miles hardly noticing it.

Our *Coolies* Break Their Contract

Few pilgrims starting out are met on this part of the return route, but *coolies* going to Badrinath take this shorter way if not accompanying pilgrims. We came across a party of eight *coolies*, in two groups of four, carrying two large bells for the temple at Badrinath, and later met 24 *coolies* carrying an enormous piece of wire cable, probably for the suspension bridge at Lambagar. Their skill at manoeuvring these difficult objects up over ridges and down into the valleys always aroused my admiration.

Early one morning we stopped on top of a ridge to get a final view of the snow-capped peaks, and a drink of milk and some potato fritters. I noticed some *sadhus* begging from some poor pilgrims. I pointed out to them that they were begging from poor pilgrims who had saved for years to be able to come on this journey, and scarcely had enough for themselves let alone provide for lazy people who only begged from others. The *sadhus* did not like it, but the pilgrims appreciated it, and as I was nearing the journey's end, I gave the *sadhus* a full dose of my mind.

The hotter it became as we neared the plains, the more energetic Khushilal became, whereas it had the reverse effect on me. After the midday break Khushilal was off again while it was still hot and I followed later. I had not gone far before I noticed dark clouds approaching from behind. They obscured the sun for which I was thankful, but I was also anxious as a heavy storm seemed imminent. I was too tired to quicken my pace. Lightning flashed and thunder rolled and I was caught in a heavy downpour. I made for the shelter of the nearest house, and was welcomed kindly by the owner, a Brahman, and his family. The rain fell heavily for half an hour and it was useless to think of venturing out while it lasted.

After the storm I went on to Srinagar. The post office was closed but the postmaster told me there were no letters. Srinagar is unpleasantly hot in June, and the Mission workers move to their headquarters at Pauri during the worst of the heat. We knew the guest house would be closed, but went straight there and occupied the verandah, which gave us all the shelter we needed. My foot still needed treatment, so as soon as I could I went next door to the government hospital, where in the absence of the doctor the compounder did what he could for me, cleaning up the sore places and binding me up with fresh lint and bandages.

Srinagar is the one and only place on the pilgrimage where it is possible to obtain meat. Khushilal is very fond of meat and had been looking forward to this treat for days. It is not possible to cook meat in the *chattis*, as the majority of pilgrims do not approve of eating meat in the neighbourhood of the sacred places. On the Amanarth pilgrimage in 1929, I was repeatedly told that the disaster that overcame the pilgrimage in 1928, when large numbers of pilgrims perished in floods and snow, was due to the Kashmiri Pandits eating chickens while on the pilgrimage.

One of the reasons for Khushilal hurrying ahead that afternoon had been to buy some meat for supper. The storm broke when he was returning from the butcher's shop. He got soaked to the skin, but had accomplished his heart's desire.

The next morning the *coolies* announced that they did not intend to go on beyond Srinagar. Raju had heard from people on the road that there was a cholera outbreak at Hardwar. I could have refused to pay the balance of what I owed him, but in some ways I was not sorry to part with them; as long as he provided a good substitute I was happy to let them go. I had already decided that I should have to engage a third *coolie*, as Raju's boils had broken out again and I was too tired to dress them every day, and for another thing I was thoroughly sick of carrying my own bundle, it being as much as I could do to carry myself along. Raju found two good strong *coolies*, who were capable of carrying all our luggage, so we paid Raju and Narayan Singh off, allowing them to keep the blankets we had bought them for the journey, and they departed satisfied to have been let off so easily.

For some days this return journey had become a matter of endurance; a daily grind that had to be got through somehow. I do not know which of us was the more tired; both equally probably. My foot had not healed, and walking had never been comfortable and the rheumatic pain in my hip, which had been troublesome in 1930, had very much increased. Restless nights, long hours on the road, the weight of my cameras and water-bottle round my neck, had all taken their toll.

As we returned to the hotter part of the road I had suffered more and more from thirst, and could never wait for the boiled water to cool. The one thing that had saved me was the success of my arrangements for making tea. I had never had another headache since I started making myself a cup of tea before starting out in the early morning.

At Devaprayag I realised that after paying off the new *coolies* I would not have sufficient money to buy our tickets home, so I had to telegraph for money to be sent to meet me at Hardwar.

The nearer we got to the end of the tramp the sooner I wanted to finish it. We spent the midday halt at Bandarbhel, where there is practically no shade. On previous journeys I had arranged to leave Bandarbhel in the early morning on account of the exhausting climb of four miles to the ridge leading over to the Hiul valley. This time we faced it at the beginning of the afternoon march with the sun full on our backs, when even hill people could not walk bare foot on the path. By taking it slowly and resting wherever there was the slightest shade, we reached the top more easily than I had expected. After that it was an easy stroll down to the PWD bungalow at Bijni, where we stayed the night.

That night I wrote to my wife what I thought would be my last letter to her before arriving back in Itarsi. The *coolies* had turned up so late with the luggage that I was having to do the best I could by candle light. Khushilal had long been asleep. I wrote: 'We have done just over 15 miles again today, including a steady ascent over the last ridge. It was a pretty stiff dose; talk about thirst. I have not recovered yet, though I have drunk gallons of water since'.

Except for the heat the last march is an easy one. Downhill for two miles, the rest mostly on the level following first the Hiul river then the Ganges. We were up before 4 a.m. and had no difficulty in reaching Garurha *chatti*, the last before Lachhman Jhula, in good time to cook our morning meal. I started again at 11.40, leaving Khushilal to bring the *coolies* in to Rishikesh, pay them off and rejoin me in Hardwar.

At Lachhman Jhula the air close to the ground was quivering with heat. I spent half an hour scrambling about the riverbanks trying to get the best view of the new suspension bridge; remembering to allow for the defects in focussing of the camera. I knew if I could sell a good postcard to Govind Prasad it would help towards paying my expenses.

I had nothing but hot water left in my water bottle and I was desperately thirsty when I reached Moni ki reti. I suddenly realised I was back to civilisation. In a ramshackle booth made of packing cases and roofed with kerosene tins, was a row of bottles containing liquid of many colours, but what was more, ICE was available for drinking purposes. After having nothing but scalding tea, plain hot or tepid water to drink for days, never has a cold drink seemed so good. Two bottles of pop with ice put new life into me.

I had hurried ahead in the hope of reaching Hardwar before the post office closed to money order business at 4 p.m. After being refreshed I found a *tonga* driver willing to take me to the motor stand at Rishikesh for two *annas*. Though it was only a short distance I had developed another thirst. A bottle-stall holder was consumed with curiosity when I urgently asked for a drink and started cross-examining me and forgot to hand over the drink, until I remarked that I could answer no questions till I had quenched my thirst.

I found a bus that would get me to Hardwar by 3 p.m. in plenty of time to collect my money. The bus was a modern Chevrolet with a powerful engine and went as fast as the road permitted. At the halfway temple we stopped to allow anyone who wished to worship and then started off again. Five miles outside Hardwar, the engine misfired and we came to a standstill; we were out of petrol. An hour later, after being left in the dust-trail of many buses, a bus of the same company came by and handed us a can of petrol. I reached the post office in Hardwar at 4.15 p.m. only to be told the money order had not arrived.

Khushilal arrived with the luggage at 7 o'clock and the train was due to leave at 10.15 p.m. I counted my money and had just enough to buy both tickets to Itarsi, leaving nothing for any extras including food or a visit to Agra. I had promised Khushilal that we would stop at Agra as he had never seen the Taj Mahal. I could not disappoint him, so I gave him enough to go to Agra alone, and saw him off on the train.

I returned to the Dak bungalow to wait as patiently as possible for the money. I could not afford English food and so had to cater for myself. Still no news of the money early next morning. I called at intervals during the day, but drew a blank each time. My stock of money was diminishing and soon I would have to pay another day's rent for my room, so I decided to pawn my cameras. I was directed to an Indian Bank and asked to see the manager. I told him what I thought my cameras were worth, and to my surprise he accepted my statement without demur and advanced me Rs.25. With intense relief I realised I was once more free to go where I wanted.

It was one more small experience by which I learnt something of what it feels like to be stranded without money, and it led me to be more sympathetic towards the many folk I have had dealings with in the course of many years in India; even though I have generally found out afterwards that my sympathy was misplaced.

In spite of this delay in Hardwar, I just succeeded in reaching Hoshangabad on Saturday afternoon, which was the latest I had allowed myself. Back in Nagpur I worked out I had lost 8½lbs in weight; it took me just a month to recover it.

Interlude: Release?

'The supreme reward of the pilgrimage is the Acquisition of God (*Bhagwatprapti*) and acquisition of the love of God (*Bhagwat prem*). In whom all the qualities of a true pilgrim are united, he will certainly obtain the supreme reward. The fruit gained by pilgrimage is so great that its equivalent cannot be obtained by sacrifices nor by offerings to Brahmans. Those in whom there is no real enthusiasm, who go on pilgrimage with purpose to commit sin, whose minds are full of doubt, who are atheists, who only go for the sake of seeing the world or for enjoyment, or for any selfish motive, and who wander among the places of pilgrimage, will never gain the supreme reward of the acquisition of God.'

(Skand Purana: Kashi: 6/35)

I HAVE OFTEN BEEN asked what are the aims and the motives of the pilgrims? What do they hope to gain from the pilgrimage? Do they achieve what they hope for? Does it bring them satisfaction? The questions are not easily answered. It is not easy to arrive at what is in another person's mind and avoid substituting what one thinks is believed for what actually is believed.

I have searched the Hindu scriptures extensively for clues that might reveal the thoughts and beliefs that are in the pilgrims' minds when they undertake these pilgrimages; beliefs that give them the courage, endurance and determination to reach their goal. The absorbing aim of the genuine Hindu pilgrim is summed up in one word – *mukti* or *moksh* – both mean the same, emancipation or release. This is not so much liberation from sin, as liberation from the fruit of actions, good or bad, performed in a previous existence, and necessitating the frequent return to this world in some form or other; the constant round of 8,400,000 rebirths, to which the Hindu must look forward under the law of Karma.

How can Release be obtained? The Hindu pilgrim believes that the rivers of India and the Ganges *par excellence*, are goddesses in whom this liberation-bestowing power is inherent. Whoever sincerely and devotedly makes right use of the sacred water of the Ganges will never be entangled in the cycle of rebirths.

This spiritual benefit is obtained in various ways and in varying degrees; by the remembrance of the Ganges in the mind, helped by repetition of the name, either mentally or aloud; by the *darshan* – the vision of God; by drinking the water and bathing in the sacred stream. Not only the person who performs these meritorious acts is benefited, but the blessings extend to his departed ancestors for several generations.

After my first journey I could almost have written myself words I found in *Nanda Devi* by E. Shipton, describing the impression the pilgrims made on him: '... the complete apathy that most pilgrims betrayed. Here was no "Happy Band of Pilgrims", but a procession of woebegone miseries that reminded us of refugees driven from their homes by an invader. None seemed to derive any pleasure from the performance of a duty which meant the principal thing in life, or from the glorious scenery through which the duty led them. One and all went along with downcast head ...'

F.S. Smythe in his book *The Valley of Flowers* seems to penetrate nearer the truth when he says: 'Something sustains these pilgrims; few seem to enjoy their pilgrimage, yet their faces are intent, their minds set on the goal ... So the pilgrimage becomes an adventure. Unknown dangers threaten the broad well made path; at any moment the gods, who hold the rocks in leash, may unloose their wrath upon the passer-by. To the European it is a walk to Badrinath; to the Hindu pilgrim it is far, far more'.

How are we to account for the prevailing gloom and downcast appearance of this long procession of pilgrims? You may go day after day and never hear a hearty laugh; never see a smile unless you provoke it yourself. There is no denying they do not appear to be a 'Happy Band of Pilgrims'.

Especially on my third journey I began to realise just how 'far, far more' it was for the pilgrim; with scarcely a day's relief from the misery of my feet; sores turning septic, low fever making me feel limp and Khushilal's illness making me doubt the wisdom of going on. I shall never forget the torture of the last climb to

Kedarnath; the weakness of my legs and back – of dragging one leg after the other, the crushing burden of the bundle over my shoulder, the ghastly nausea and lack of will power to vomit and gain relief, the biting wind and stinging sleet on my face and bare arms; all reduced me to a state when I cared little whether I reached the top or even saw my home again. In those few hours, and in other painful experiences, I entered as never before into sympathy with the sufferings of many of my fellow pilgrims, whose gloom I had been too ready to attribute to other causes.

On the outward journey there were many opportunities of talking to the pilgrims, and sometimes I tried to discover their real thoughts concerning the pilgrimage. Many educated men frankly admitted they had no faith in it; some saying they came to avoid the hot weather on the plains and thought they might combine seeing the sacred places and taking a holiday; others said they had been ill and had come for a change; others had come because their womenfolk believed in it, so they came to look after them.

The strong faith of the simple-minded villagers was remarkable. Though they listened willingly to what we had to say, it was evident they saw no reason to be other than satisfied with their own ancestral belief. Even when we met them coming down footsore and faint, impoverished and disheartened, they still clung to the hope that in the next rebirth they would reap the benefit of their suffering.

On the homeward journey ourselves, the opportunities to talk intimately with pilgrims are few. Their objectives have been attained, the ceremonies performed, the vision of God granted, the *panda's* demands satisfied, and now they want to get home as quickly as possible, before their remaining money and strength are exhausted. Besides, we ourselves were tired and not in the mood for talking after a long day's march.

One day I overtook a man who was hobbling along with his feet bound up in rags. We began to talk and he told me he was a Brahman from the United Provinces. He was very depressed, and when I asked him to tell me frankly what he thought, he replied: 'I have spent all my money, I have performed all the ceremonies that I was told to do, I am physically worn out, and in return I have gained absolutely nothing'.

There is a word the pilgrims use to describe the success or otherwise of the pilgrimage – *saphal*. It translates, successful, auspicious, fruitful, fulfilled. It is a word *pandas* know well how to use to squeeze more money out of their patrons, by saying 'your pilgrimage will be fruitless'. When I asked 'Has your pilgrimage been successful?', as likely as not I got the stock answer 'Ram jane' (God knows). There was no joyful certainty, but a kind of dogged fatalism that said, 'I have done all I know and now must leave it; only in the next incarnation shall I find out'. They had performed all the ceremonies, bowed at every shrine, left their offerings of grain and flowers, money according to their means and they could do no more.

For these we had a message that the mercy and forgiveness of God were not dependent on any works of our own, nor merit that we could accumulate, but were free to all through the merit of Jesus Christ, in whom the Father was well pleased because He completely fulfilled the Father's will.

Over and over again I was asked 'Have you had the *darshan*?' and I would reply, 'Not the kind of *darshan* you mean. I do not seek that kind of *darshan* as I have seen the glory of God in the face of Jesus Christ. The real *darshan* is something you and I and every-one may have within our own minds, every day, anywhere. "He that hath seen me hath seen the Father"'.

Talking to pilgrims it often seemed natural and fitting to bring the conversation round to the story of the woman at the well, and pass on what one felt Christ himself would have said. 'Fellow pilgrim, believe me, the hour cometh when neither in this moun-tain nor in that, will men worship the Father. Ye worship that which ye know not; we worship that which we know. But the hour cometh, and now is, when the true worshippers shall worship the Father in spirit and in truth; for such doth the Father seek to be his wor-shippers. God is a spirit, and they that worship him must worship in spirit and truth.'

Surely it was no mere fancy that we had as our companion, an unseen pilgrim on the road. One who, 'when he saw the multitudes was moved with compassion'. It was he who had said, 'Foxes have holes, and the birds of the heaven have nests, but the Son of Man hath not where to lay his head', and who knew the meaning of hard-ship and suffering; hunger, thirst and weariness, but nevertheless 'steadfastly set his face to go to Jerusalem'. Surely his spirit was not far from the ragged and footsore pilgrims as they toiled along the rocky path, and as they stretched their weary bodies on the hard ground at night; as they bathed in the rivers, and bowed their heads in the temples in their search for release and peace.

PART V
THE 1948 PILGRIMAGE

CHAPTER 7

Farewell to an Adventure

'It is an ancient custom to perform the pilgrimage on foot. In the old days, lovers of pilgrimages, men and women, set out with high enthusiasm, banded together, and with no expectation of returning. At that time there were no railways, motors, or other conveyances. The pilgrim band endured heat and rain. But their enthusiasm was so great that their suffering was changed to joy.'

'Those pilgrims who travel by bullock cart shall live for many days in hell; their ancestors cannot accept the holy water they offer, and the fruit of their pilgrimage is destroyed. Those who go on pilgrimage on foot, their sins diminish at every step, and they participate in special reward. On pilgrimage one should not travel very fast nor very slowly, but should leave home filled with joy in the company of worthy people.'

(Markandeya Rishi to Yuddhishthir)

IN 1948 I DID A shortened pilgrimage, going by bus and lorry along the new motor road which then reached as far as Nandprayag. I was very glad of this saving of time and labour, as I did not have the time to do the full pilgrimage, and was anxious to have a longer stay in Badrinath to contact various old friends. Above all arthritis which on earlier pilgrimages had given me increasing pain, had reached the stage that it had immobilised one hip, and the full journey would have been physically impossible for me. So this meant the 450-mile walk was reduced to a mere 108 miles. Nevertheless I am glad to have known the pilgrimage in the days when it was a full physical feat of walking on foot.

142

By 1948 other circumstances had changed. The Second World
War had affected the pilgrimage in many ways. The cost of living
had increased and wages of *coolies* risen in proportion. Chiefly for
this reason I was obliged to undertake the journey alone, leaving
my faithful companion Khushilal behind. I wore European dress,
and found this led to no serious difficulties either in making friends
with the pilgrims or living in the *chattis*, and it gave me greater freedom for photography.

What do the saints and sages think who are said to have spent
thousands of years in meditation in these valleys, if from the untrou-
bled calm of the celestial regions they can see the cavalcade of motor
vehicles, careering round the corners of the narrow road, while
humble pilgrims who still travel on foot cling anxiously to crevices
in the rocks by the roadside and inhale petrol fumes and clouds of
dust that linger long after the modern car of Jagannath has passed
on its way? If Markandeya Rishi taught that pilgrims who travelled
in bullock carts forfeited their hopes of heaven, what would he have
said to the modern pilgrims who reduce the rigour of the pilgrimage by travelling most of the way by means of 'railways, motors and
other conveyances', and even by aeroplane?

When I decided to make my fourth and final trip, the bus service was struggling with post-war difficulties. The management
could not guarantee that one would arrive at the place mentioned
on the ticket, and it was impossible to keep to a regular timetable.
Enough passengers besieged the ticket offices to fill treble the
number of buses available. Petrol frequently ran short, and no-one
knew when the next lot would be delivered. Tyres burst and could
not be replaced, and spare parts were almost unprocurable.

After losing a whole day at Kotdwara, the railway terminus on
the plains, I was eventually given a seat on a bus through the kindness of someone of influence, although other people had been waiting longer than I had. By late afternoon we reached Pauri and were
told we would go no further. However the next morning I was given
a seat in another bus and warned that I might not be taken further
than Karnprayag.

From Pauri the road zig-zags down the steep sides of the valley
by a series of hairpin bends to the Alaknanda valley, emerging below
Srinagar. Between Srinagar and Rudraprayag the road deviates
from the old pilgrim path and instead of climbing up and down

several ridges, is cut out of the precipitous hillside close to the river. At Rudraprayag several buses were waiting to pass. The road is so narrow with dangerous corners and bends that a system of one-way traffic is in operation. At Rudraprayag a great crowd of passengers thronged the numerous teashops. The teashop trade was a new development. Instead of a limited supply of milk quickly bought up by lucky pilgrims, there now seemed to be enough for tea for everyone at almost any time of day. It was the one thing on the road that was reasonably cheap – two *annas* for a brass tumblerful.

On reaching Karnprayag I was told the bus would go no further. The temporary bridge over the Pindari river was not safe and moreover there was no petrol. There might be a road contractor's lorry on the other side which would take a load of passengers to Nandprayag, but meantime there was no alternative but to stop the night. I secured a room in the Public Works Department bungalow and arranged for my meals from a shopkeeper near the footbridge. Next morning I was promised a seat next to the driver of the contractor's lorry, and told we would be leaving in the afternoon. While waiting at the booking office I noticed a man in saffron clothes and went across to speak to him. He was from Benares and had been appointed as the new Vedpathi to join the Rawal Sahib and accompany him to Badrinath. A Vedpathi's duty is to chant the Vedas in the temple while the Rawal Sahib performs the daily worship. His full name and title was Agnihotri Pandit Agnishwatta Shastri. He told me the Rawal Sahib was waiting at a nearby village and was also hoping to go on the first available transport to Nandprayag.

The contractor's lorry arrived earlier than expected and I received short notice to fetch my luggage from the bungalow, and have it transported to the other side of the river. I found the Rawal Sahib had forestalled me and was already settled in the driver's cab. So I proceeded to prepare as comfortable and safe a seat as possible on top of the mound of loose luggage in the back of the lorry, along with the Vedpathi and about 20 other passengers. The luggage was not secured by ropes and there was nothing to hang onto except the smooth surface of the roof of the driver's cab. The road had only recently been opened to motor traffic and the surface was covered with loose metal and even small boulders. There was nothing to prevent us going over the edge, and it was so narrow that from my perch there appeared nothing between me and the water some hundreds of feet below. At each corner we were in imminent danger of being shot off our precarious perch. The lorry had no horn, but 'audible notice of approach' was provided by the conductor who rode on the driver's running board, and rendered a perfect imitation of a Klaxon horn.

It was dark by the time we reached Nandprayag, half a mile below the town near the suspension bridge over the Mandakini river. I found a couple of *coolies* to carry my luggage and guide me up the unlighted path to the house of my old friend Pandit Govind Prasad Nautiyal who kindly gave me a good meal and a room for the night. The Rawal Sahib and the Vedpathi were entertained by Govind Prasad's uncle, Seth Shankar Datt, the leading Brahman of that place.

I was told that only a few days before, when the first summer residents were making arrangements to re-occupy their summer houses and shops in Badrinath, there had been a disastrous avalanche which had wiped out nearly half the town. Eighty-four houses had been demolished or buried beneath débris, but the temple and 112 other houses were still intact. Fortunately the disaster occurred just before the season began, so there was no loss of life. Warnings were issued in newspapers throughout India to try and persuade people not to undertake the pilgrimage, as inevitably they would have to endure more hardship than usual, but pilgrims were already making their way up. Local authorities were straining every nerve to restore the town and provide accommodation for 1,500 permanent residents and an influx of a thousand pilgrims a day.

One immediate result was a scarcity of *coolies* – all available men were urgently called to Badrinath where higher wages could be earned than by carrying luggage for pilgrims. Even the Rawal Sahib had difficulty in getting away the next morning, while I was stranded. I spent the next four days in the old PWD bungalow by the bus stand while the transport officer made enquiries about *coolies* for me. The delay was very tantalising as it was hot down near the river and there was a plague of flies in the bungalow. I thought I knew all the twelve plagues of the pilgrim road, but I discovered a thirteenth. Sacks of wheat were piled up in all the rooms and millions of weevils had sprung to life and swarmed everywhere – my trunk and bedding and everything I picked up was covered with them. Had they now come on a vast pilgrimage to the holy Ganges in the hope of coming back in human form? Some went on a long trip with me and eventually found themselves on the plains of Central India. Finally, when not even the local transport officer seemed able to produce *coolies* for me, I found a ponyman, Renu, and decided to engage him.

Engaging a ponyman instead of two *coolies* was a new experience for me, but there seemed no alternative. Renu was a Dhotiyal, belonging to a hill caste not reckoned high in the social scale. I bargained with him to carry my luggage from Nandprayag to Badrinath – a distance of 54 miles for Rs.40. I was to provide morning tea and refreshments. He was supposed to pay for the pony's grass, but in practice I generally did when the pony could not graze for itself. He was not allowed to sleep in the same place as the *coolies*, being from a lower caste, and sometimes pleaded loneliness at night and begged to be allowed to share my room when I used the engineers' bungalows – which was against the rules.

It takes two people to load and unload a pony, and as Renu had no companion I had to help him and learn the special ways that hillmen know of tying burdens on so that they cannot slip or cut into the pony's belly. One difficulty was that my basket containing my primus stove, and a pail which I considered indispensable, could not be easily attached to the rest of the load, and were in constant danger of dropping off or being crushed against the mountainside.

Several times Renu had to cook for both of us, and to contribute something on loan from his private store of rice and lentils, and I would have gone hungry except for his co-operation. I did feel somewhat aggrieved that after having had nothing to eat all day, I was given only the merest taste of the half cabbage that a young Brahman sub-overseer of the PWD, J.C. Joshi, had contributed to my larder because he found that I had been getting such poor fare at the teashop.

Almost every day Renu harrowed my feelings by telling me of conversations with his acquaintances who expressed their disapproval that he was helping an Englishman get to Badrinath. He claimed they had threatened him and suggested he find an opportunity of disposing of my luggage by tipping it over some precipice into the river. This would have been difficult without also sending the pony to certain death – but not impossible. He kept assuring me that he had stoutly resisted the suggestion, but I was acutely aware of how much depended on his loyalty. My peace of mind was completely ruined when he threatened to leave me. However, it never got further than grumbling and in the end he fulfilled his contract. After I paid him off he returned to his winter home near Nandprayag. I met him again on my way back, when he was on his way to his summer home on the eastern side of Gauri Parbat. He had exchanged his white pony for a bullock, which did not appear to me to be an advantage.

It was good to be back on the pilgrim path again, and soon we were at Chamoli. At a corner in the pine forest I stopped to take a photograph, but it needed human interest, so I waited. Along came a tall old man dressed in saffron clothes. I stopped him and found he was an old soldier and proud of his service for the British Raj. Now in his old age he was visiting the holy places. I asked him if he would be in my picture and immediately he placed his bundle on the ground, stood to attention as stiff as a ramrod and shouldered his stick as if it had been a rifle. I pretended to take the photo, then as he stopped to pick up his bundle, caught him in a typical pilgrim posture, just what I wanted.

A remarkable pilgrim who attracted my attention was a tall distinguished-looking man dressed in one flowing white sheet. He was bareheaded, and though sunburnt obviously not an Indian. He told me he was a follower of the Jain religion. He spoke English with a continental accent and on being pressed admitted to being Swiss. I asked if he had renounced the Christian faith in favour of Jainism. He replied that he had not done so and that Christianity had nothing to be ashamed of, but he had joined up with Jainism for the practice of Yoga, without which he felt he could not attain his goal. He had been to Badrinath and was on his way back to Mount Abu. Though impressed with the scenery of the Himalayas, he said he had seen nothing to compare with the beauty of Switzerland.

Soon after passing through Patalganga, the Ganges of the Nether Regions, we had great difficulty getting the pony and baggage across a serious landslide. There had been a severe thunderstorm and heavy rain the night before. Several small landslides had

Proud old soldier.

Landslide at Patalganga, 1948.

caused gaps in the road. At a fork a notice said that laden animals should go via a diversion as the road was unsafe. People coming the other way told us it was being repaired and they thought we could get across. We decided to risk it as the diversion involved a stiff climb and several extra miles. When we reached the landslide, Renu unloaded the pony, took my bedding roll across on his head, returned for my trunk and deposited that. Then he came back and told me to take the pony's bridle, which had been thrown over its head, and lead the way while he hung onto the pony's tail and brought up the rear. On the way across he told me of a police constable and laden pony who had gone over here and been lost in the river hundreds of feet below only the previous year. We were more fortunate and managed to hold ourselves and the pony up, though the footholds were often precarious. It took a full hour to make the crossing. Returning three weeks later we found that the warning was still in force. In one place I was sheltering behind a projecting rock when the corner of a large box on a mule's back caught against it and the mule nearly went over the edge.

The annual departure of the Rawal Sahib for Badrinath early in April to open the temple after the snow has melted, marks the beginning of the pilgrimage season. For the residents of Joshimath and surrounding villages this is the great event of the year. The removal is accomplished by people called *deodharis*, who have the hereditary obligation to carry something connected with the temple to Badrinath in return for a payment of so much rice and certain village rights. I had never been in Joshimath in time to witness this event as I had always started from Hardwar and followed the longest route. On this visit I was much earlier and soon after Chamoli I fell in with two Badrinath *pandas*, the official bearers of the sacred oil provided by the Rajah of Tehri, which the Rawal Sahib takes up to Badrinath. They told me the procession would leave Joshimath the day after they arrived, so I tried to keep up with them. Owing to a heavy downpour I fell behind, but by taxing my lame leg to the limit, I arrived at noon on the day the Rawal should have left in the morning. To my great relief his departure had been postponed till 2 o'clock by an eclipse of the moon early that morning.

I enquired for the Secretary of the Badrinath Temple Committee, Shri Purushottam Bagwari. His house above the town commands a wonderful view. Directly in front the shining peaks of

Gauri Parbat and Hathi Parbat dominate the whole picture. The sheer mountain walls on the left are broken by the deep narrow valley of the Alaknanda and on the right by the similar valley of the Dhauli river. I found the Secretary with several of the local gentry making their preparations to join the Rawal Sahib's party. I was unable after the morning's effort to accompany the procession myself as I would have liked, but the Secretary kindly placed his house at my disposal and left me with vacant possession.

By 2 o'clock a crowd had collected near the temple and the weird sounds of drums and musical instruments floated up the hillside. I joined the crowd expectantly waiting for the Rawal to emerge. Presently the beat of drums became louder and out of the wide doorway came the standard-bearer followed by the drummers and men bearing great curly trumpets. Then two scarlet-coated *chaprasis* carrying heavy silver maces. After them came the palanquin with a gay purple top, in which the Rawal Sahib was seated; by his side were liveried servants waving yak-tail fly-whisks – the sign of his high priestly rank. As the procession came out of the last of the five temples where the Rawal Sahib had made his final acts of worship, I asked if he would remain standing on the steps while

Rawal Sahib and temple officials leaving Joshimath for Badrinath.

I took a photograph. That over, he re-entered his palanquin, the procession re-formed, and to the sound of trumpets and drums, marched off down the steep path to Vishnuprayag.

Thanking me later for sending him copies of the photos, he replied, '... they are really nice. They will remind me of your good company'.

My three previous visits to Badrinath were of necessity short – the longest being four whole days. This last visit I was able to stay for 12 nights. I was unable to stay with my friend Seth Shankar Datt as he was expecting his own family, so had to seek other shelter. I found a charitable organisation, the Panjab Sindh Kshetra, had moved into a new building three-quarters of a mile from the temple. A venerable grey-bearded gentleman wearing sunglasses, whom I took to be the manager, was standing close by. When I enquired if he could give me a room, his generous response warmed my heart. I was shown to one of the two best rooms reserved for special guests. It had a window with wooden shutters facing the town. The only furniture was a bedstead of solid wooden planks, which I found very hard.

Pandit Jagat Ram, the manager, willingly offered to provide me with food in the mornings, along with the *sadhus* who came for free meals. He would not accept money, so I told him I would send a donation to the institution's headquarters after I returned home. I would buy my evening meal from one of the shops in town. As it happened I had a mild attack of malaria during my stay and on the evenings when my temperature was up, Pandit Jagat Ram had rice and lentils specially cooked for me, as that was unobtainable in town. I noticed how loved and respected Jagat Ram was by the *sadhus*. He told me he had been a pupil of the famous 'Dr Pennell of the Afghan Frontier', and from him he had caught his ideal of service for humanity.

There were several *sadhus* staying at the *kshetra*, among them one called Abdhut Baba, whose fame had spread beyond Badrinath. I had several opportunities of watching and listening while he talked to other visitors as he sat in the sun on the grass in the sheltered courtyard. He wore only a small strip of cloth, a brass *lota* and a pair of tongs were his only possessions. If he used a blanket at night it was borrowed from the *kshetra*. He had come over from Gangotri

*G. W.M. with
Abdhut Baba
above Badrinath.*

in that condition, a five-day journey over the snow, crossing a pass which is rarely traversed by ordinary mortals.

After two days I was offered an upper room in a house belonging to Seth Shankar Datt, across the road from his own house. This had a *charpoy* strung with webbing which was softer than my wooden bed. Pandit Jagat Ram did not take offence at my going, and continued to supply my needs. From three windows I could now watch all the comings and goings of the pilgrim road. On the ground floor a family of Marchhas were living, and the little girl with her baby brother on her hip was always about outside, frequently begging from the pilgrims. Below one window was a wide stone platform, and a drinking place where water was brought by pipe from a mile up the mountainside. Here exhausted pilgrims often stayed to drink and rest, disinclined to rise and finish their journey.

Soon after it was light the procession began with pilgrims arriving who had left Hanuman *chatti* while it was still dark. There were poor pilgrims carrying their own burdens; some with bundles on their heads, some with a *khariya* (double bag) slung over their shoulders; some with blankets tied round their waists, or a small roll of bedding tied up in a *darri* (cotton mat) under their arms. Almost every pilgrim had a *lota* (brass drinking pot) in his hand and a stick to help him in climbing. Then there were the *coolies* laden with the wealthier pilgrims' luggage – trunks, bedding rolls, holdalls, pails, tins, wooden boxes, sacks and bags; there were *coolies* carrying pilgrims in *dandis*, *jhampans* and *kandis*. Besides them there were the Marchha men and women from Mana village, some carrying bundles of firewood, cans of milk or bundles of grass. Even the children were carrying smaller *kandis* made to fit their smaller backs. Hundreds of animals passed below the window, ponies, mules, donkeys, bullocks and *jhabbuas* (a cross between an ox and a yak), laden with heavy packing-cases full of all kinds of things for the shops – tins of *ghi* or kerosene oil, sheets of galvanised iron and wooden planks for building and repairs. Flocks of goats with double bags of grain or sugar or salt or lentils slung across their backs, were led by three or four of the finest animals with bells round their necks, and with shepherds and sheepdogs to lead the way and to follow up the rear.

The avalanche had devastated Badrinath just as the town was about to open for the pilgrimage season. The main mass of snow had divided on reaching the town, leaving two broad paths of destruction with an island of undamaged houses between. The temple itself was undamaged as it stands on this sloping island ridge which deflected the avalanche, but many houses and shops with all their contents had been swept into the rushing waters below. All kinds of débris were piled up on the opposite side of the river. Two *pandas* I knew, on hearing I had returned, came and told me their house had been completely demolished and everything it contained ruined or destroyed.

The shopkeepers leave their unsold stock in their shops ready for the next season. Those selling perishable goods in the path of the avalanche had mostly lost it all. More fortunate was a man named Urba Datt. He had tunnelled his way into his shop, the roof of which had stood the strain, and found his stock of books, pictures, trinkets, rosaries and souvenirs undamaged. He remembered me from previous visits when Khushilal and I had bought some things from his father. In spite of the snow still piled on his roof, it was 'business as usual' inside the shop, which resembled a dug-out in a front-line trench. He insisted on entertaining me to afternoon tea. I sat in the mouth of his cave with my feet in the street, which turned out to be convenient, as he refilled my mug so often that I was able to empty the last lot into the gutter when I thought I was not observed.

One of the first people I met was the genial Secretary of the Temple Committee, Shri Purushottam Bagwari (mentioned earlier). He was superintending the army of workmen who were clearing the streets, digging out houses and rebuilding them as fast as materials could be provided. Seeing my camera the Secretary seized a shovel and struck a pose as if engaged in clearing the snow. It does not take an expert to see he was more used to handling a pen than a spade. To me he was kindness personified. Twice he sent me tray-loads of food prepared by the temple cooks, served on solid silver dishes, and of a quality unobtainable in the bazaar. He was quite hurt when I did not appeal to him to make arrangements to transport my luggage back to Nandprayag.

Ganga Par

It is emphasised in the Hindu scriptures that those whose aim is the attainment of God (*Bhagwatprapti*) and the love of God (*Bhagwatprem*) should retire from all else and become attached to God. This is accomplished by the companionship of God-loving great souls found at the holy places. Association with these good and pious persons (*satsang*) is a duty enjoined on pilgrims, who therefore seek the society and instructions of *sadhus* who have 'arrived', or who have 'attained perfection'.

The left bank of the Alaknanda opposite the town is known as Ganga Par (across the Ganges). Great rocks stick out and built between them are little shelters, which are the *sadhu's* 'hermitages'. Some of the buildings actually fit into the curves of the rocks which form part of the walls or roof. Some are caves fitted with a façade and lock-up door. The noise and clamour of the bazaar is drowned by the ceaseless roar of the river as it cascades against the rocks. The temple bell carries across as each pilgrim pulls the clapper rope, announcing his desire for *darshan*. The square gold-covered roof of the main temple reflects the last of the sunlight till darkness falls.

Further back from the steep banks the roar of water fades to a gentle murmur. On the hillside all is quiet and peaceful. *Sadhus* sit meditating outside in the sunshine, seeking self-realisation through union of the soul with the Universal Spirit. All systems of Indian philosophy aim to emancipate the soul through perfection, uniting the soul, literally, with the One Soul.

One afternoon I set out on an adventure of friendship. The footpath led past several cottages with locked doors – some on the outside, some from the inside. Through an open door I saw a *sadhu* with a great mane of hair. I later came to know him as Vimalananda. He was not meditating and invited me to come inside. A friend presently joined us and we sat talking. The friend started fishing around in a cloth bag and brought out a handful of mixed nuts and sultanas which he shared round, in the way that *sadhus* and others, who have no tea to offer, fulfil the courtesy of hospitality which according to Indian custom must be extended to visitors, and without which no caller can be dismissed. Vimalananda remarked that I would probably be interested in meeting another *sadhu*, who, he said, was translating Thomas à Kempis' *The Imitation of Christ* into Bengali. The friend guided me to another cottage. The door was shut from the inside, but in answer to a knock, a *sadhu* appeared whom I had previously noticed carrying food away from the Panjab Sindh Kshetra when I had been there for the same purpose. I apologised for disturbing his meditations, but he invited me in. This was the beginning of a lasting friendship. Shri Hari Narayan Basu was an M.Sc. of Calcutta University. During the second war, under the British Government he had worked as a textile engineering expert. After the war he accepted a job in a new textile mill, with excellent prospects and a salary of Rs.2,000 per month. This did not satisfy his spiritual aspirations and he gave it all up to devote his whole mind to the search for emancipation. He was unmarried and had left his home and parents so that he might pursue his search undisturbed. He did not beg, though accepted food when offered. If he needed money he gave tuition for just the amount required. His only possessions were the thin white cotton clothes he was wearing, one spare cloth, two blankets (one of which he gave away when he returned to the plains), his brass *lota*, and three books, one of which was *The Imitation of Christ*.

When I remarked that this custom of *sadhus* renouncing the world and going off to meditate in solitude to attain union with the Ultimate Reality seemed selfish to Westerners, he was quite hurt. He assured me that many *sadhus* pursued their search for truth with unselfish motives, and as they realised their union with God, became capable of sending forth powerful radiation of peace and so contribute to overcoming evil in the world.

One of my happiest memories is of an old *sannyasi* named Swami Dhyan Sarup. Hari Narayan Basu told me that he often talked to this wise old man who was reputed to have arrived at the stage of *siddhi* or perfection. I first made his acquaintance early one morning when I passed near his cottage, 'Shanti Kuti' (Peace Cottage). It was surrounded by a wall on which I sat in the sunshine while he entertained me. He found the cold dry climate and lack of fats in my diet was affecting my health, and he was determined to rectify that. He brewed a strong tumblerful of tea, added a generous quantity of sugar and powdered ginger. On top of this was floating an inch of *ghi*. For the sake of friendship I have

Badrinath temple from Ganga Par. Swami Dhyan Sarup.

accustomed myself to eating and drinking many things from which the fastidious would shrink, but this was a severe test of the stability of my stomach. The ginger however makes a good substitute for milk.

The last time I 'enjoyed' his hospitality, the test was not quite so severe. Along with the ginger-flavoured tea he produced a quarter of a pound of congealed *ghi* in the middle of a *chapati* from which he had broken off all the edges in case they were too dry and tough. With the help of another *chapati* I was able to swallow and retain the *ghi*.

Outside the garden wall was a carpet of blue and purple wild dwarf iris, which daily became more brilliant as the buds responded to the warmth of the sun. There were many other flowers coming out among the grass and in the damper places the ground was covered with tiny bees that had come to drink, and it seemed impossible to walk without crushing them. The *swami* assured me that they were so sensitive that they escaped before we could tread on them. When discussing *himsa* and *ahimsa* (the taking of life and non-violence) I raised the question of killing snakes and other poisonous and harmful creatures. The *swami* replied that for one seeking unity with the Ultimate Reality there was no fear of harm, and he told me from his own experience accounts of how snakes had crawled over him while he was meditating, and of his having completely lost all fear.

In contrast I met one afternoon outside the temple a *sadhu* youth adorned with a garland of human skulls. I watched him drink some tea given to him by a shopkeeper from his begging bowl which was the top of another skull. There are three sects whose members worship Shiva in his 'dreadful' form, and wear human skulls – the Kapalikas, the Kalamukhs and the Aghoris, to which I supposed this youth belonged. *Sadhus* of the Aghori path pursue the doctrine of the all-pervadingness of God to its utmost, and argue that human flesh and filth are thus pervaded and can be eaten. To prove this they are prepared to eat human flesh from the burning *ghats*. While I was sitting at a shop, the youth came across followed by an admiring crowd and made silly faces. Later I heard of him again from the temple Secretary. Shri Purushottam Bagwari had been standing below the tower of the temple of Lakshman, when the youth entered the courtyard like any other pilgrim seeking the *darshan*.

For no apparent reason the flag from the tower fell between them and the *pandas* assumed that the deity objected to the youth's presence, and he was hustled out of the courtyard.

The sacred food offered to the god in the temple is known as *Mahaprasad*, and partaking of it is an important rite of the pilgrimage. Badrinath shares with the sacred place of Jagannath Puri in Orissa the distinction of being a place where the rules regarding loss of caste by contamination from eating with other people are in abeyance. All caste Hindus are freed from the fear of contamination while in Badrinath. Many pilgrims carry home sun-dried portions of *Mahaprasad* for distribution to their relatives, as 'its properties are so wonderful, that even if an outcaste were to touch it, he would be respected by every caste in India', according to a little book entitled *The Call of Badrinath*, published in English and Hindi by my friend Pandit Govind Prasad Nantiyal, who owns a shop and Shilajit factory in Nandprayag. Having procured some of this sacred *Bhog*, together with some other ingredients, the pilgrim accompanied by his *panda* is taken to Brahma Kapal (Skull of Brahma) for the final and most important ceremony. Brahma Kapal is a huge rock jutting out into the river 200 yards upstream; part of the rock bears some resemblance to a skull. The platform, artificially enlarged, is approached through a door in a wall. At the entrance a perpetual fire is burning and the smell of incense fills the air. The pilgrims prepare their offerings and when all the names of the departed have been recited, prayers and mantras said, the offerings are thrown into the sacred stream. Food and gifts are then given to the officiating Brahmans, who give the assurance that the ceremony will be efficacious. Badrinath is one of the few places in India where the performance of *Shraddh* is so efficacious that it does not have to be repeated. When that is completed the pilgrim turns his face homeward.

Before leaving Badrinath I paid a final visit to Brahma Kapal. A *panda* was sitting on the ground outside the door, with a bulky register open in front of him. By his side was a wooden box in which he kept his pens and ink and the pepper-castor containing fine black sand, which serves the purpose of blotting paper. As the pilgrims emerged from the door, the *panda* invited them to have their names entered in his register; for this service he made a small charge of one *anna* per name. Some of the pilgrims, who felt that

Brahm Kapal.

the ceremony had already involved them in sufficient expense, tried to evade this further imposition, but the *panda* had a persuasive way, and his argument that without this final act the whole performance would just fail to be efficacious, usually overcame the pilgrims' hesitancy.

I asked this *panda* when the time would come that Gandhiji's ideal would be fulfilled and Badrinath temple, like many other temples in India, would be made accessible to the untouchables. He replied, that soon the untouchables might be granted the right of temple entry in theory, under the constitution, but the *pandas* had their own methods by which to render the law a dead letter.

This conversation took place a few weeks after Gandhiji's assassination, and his ashes were at that very time being distributed among all the sacred places for casting into the sacred rivers. The bearers arrived only a few days after I left and were to have taken the ashes 12 miles beyond Badrinath to be scattered in the sacred lake of Satopanth, the real source of the Alaknanda. They were however, scattered on the water at Badrinath. Members of the

Temple Committee and all the gentry of Garwal accompanied the procession, and a great public meeting was held at which the resolution was solemnly accepted that in memory of Gandiji the temple should henceforth be open to the untouchables. I do not know to what extent this resolution has become effective.

Among the women pilgrims there was one I noticed several times. She had only one leg, and walked with the aid of a rough pair of unpadded crutches, simply a couple of bamboos stuck into two blocks of wood to go under her arms. I overtook her between Pandukeshwar and Joshimath and stopped to talk. She had been a factory-worker in Calcutta, and had to have her leg amputated abcve the knee as the result of an accident. I last saw her swinging along into Karnprayag just as I was leaving. She was only 12 hours behind me and had travelled 56 miles of which I had done the last 12 by bus.

A resident whom I remember with affection was a Brahman youth named Satyeshwar Prasad Sati. He attached himself to me as a voluntary guide while I was waiting for the bus at Karnprayag. He had qualified sufficiently from the local High School to be a teacher in a hill-village school. His father, a farmer, was now getting past working and Satyeshwar had to support his parents and several younger children. His meeting with me had aroused the hope that I might be the means of his liberation. Regretfully I had to tell him that I would soon be leaving India and had no work to offer him. He helped fetch my luggage down to the bus and refused all payment – not even a cup of tea at my expense. As the bus drove off in a cloud of dust, I could see him still standing disconsolately by the side of the road.

In looking back over my experiences it is a pleasure to be able to say that by the hosts of people whom I met, of all classes and conditions, with very rare exceptions, so rare as to be practically negligible, I was treated with nothing but kindness and sympathy, and in many cases with something amounting even to affection. The vast majority seemed distinctly pleased that an Englishman should mix with them on such free and familiar terms. So many little acts of courtesy made the pilgrimage an unforgettable experience, and more than made up for any unpleasantnesses and inconveniences.

Wherever I have told the story of the pilgrimage the words of St Paul to the Christians at Rome come to mind. 'Brethren, my heart's desire and my supplication to God is for them, that they may be saved. For I bear them witness that they have a zeal for God, but not according to knowledge. For being ignorant of God's righteousness, and seeking to establish their own, they did not subject themselves to the righteousness of God. For there is no distinction, for the same Lord is Lord of all, and is rich unto all that call upon him. How then shall they call on him in whom they have not believed? and how shall they believe in him whom they have not heard? and how shall they hear without a preacher?'

Glossary

Advaita	Non-duality
Ahimsa	Doctrine of non-violence
Anna	Coin equal to about one penny (in the 1930s)
Ashram	Hermitage; place of retreat for religious group
Bakshish	Gratuity; reward
Bhog	Food offered to an idol
Chamar	Leather worker; shoemaker
Chapati	Thin cake of unleavened bread
Chaprasi	Messenger wearing a badge
Chaprasin	School servant, whose duty it is to chaperone girls to school
Charpoy	Bedstead, woven with string or tape
Chatti	Shelter, or groups of shelters where pilgrims rest, cook and sleep
Chela	Disciple
Chirr Pine	Tree resembling a Scots Pine
Chini	Sugar
Chit	Testimonial letter
Chota Haziri	Early morning tea, little breakfast
Dak bungalow	Travellers' rest-house
Dandi	Chair carried by four coolies
Darri	Cotton Carpet
Darshan	Viewing and worshipping in the presence of an image
Dharmshala	Rest-house erected and maintained by charitable funds

Dhoti	Man's waist cloth
Diksha	Initiation; receiving of initiatory mantra
Ekadasi	Eleventh day of a lunar fortnight
Ekka	Conveyance drawn by one pony
Ghat	Bathing steps leading to water's edge; mountain pass
Ghi (ghee)	Clarified butter
Gumastar	Panda's agent
Guru	Spiritual teacher
Haqq	Righteous due
Hartal	Strike; cessation of business as a protest
Himsa	The taking of life
Huqah	Tobacco pipe; smoke drawn through water
Jalebi	Sweetmeat
Jhampan	String seat carried by four coolies
Jhula	Suspension bridge; swing
Kachhi	Market gardener
Kalikamliwala	Belonging to sect of 'Saint with a Black Blanket'
Kandi	Coolie's basket, used to carry a load or person on the back
Khaddar	Homespun cotton cloth
Khansama	Caretaker of Dak bungalow
Khariya	Double bag made of cloth for carrying over the shoulder
Khichari	Lentils and rice boiled together
Khidmatgar	Table waiter
Kilta	Kashmiri wicker basket
Kshattriya	Ruling caste; warrior
Kurta	Garment like a long shirt
Lakh	100,000
Lingam	Phallic emblem of Shiva
Lota	Small brass pot

Mahabharat	Epic Poem; attributed to Vyasji, describing wars of Kurus and Pandavas
Mahant	Abbot; Prior of sect of ascetics
Mahaprasad	Food offered to deity and afterwards distributed
Masaks	Inflated buffalo skins
Mela	Religious Fair
Mochi	Cobbler
Mukti; Moksh	Spiritual emancipation; release
Munshi	Secretary; language teacher
Panda	Religious guide; priest presiding at a temple
Pandit	Learned man
Paratha	Unleavened cake made with ghi
Patwari	Government servant who keeps official records of land ownership
Pice	Coin of very small value
Pind shraddh	Funeral rite observed at various fixed periods
Purana	Ancient Hindu text containing stories of the gods
Prasad	Food offered to deity and afterwards distributed
Prayag	Sacred place situated at junction of two rivers
Pujari	Temple priest
Puri	Unleavened cake fried in oil or ghi
Pya-u	Drinking place where water is supplied as an act of merit
Ram	Appelation of one of the incarnations of Vishnu
Rawal	High Priest
Ringal	Plant resembling bamboo
Rupee	Silver coin worth about 1s. 6d. (in the 1930s)
Sadhu	Saint; holy man; Hindu mendicant
Sahib	Term of respect, e.g. Rawal Sahib; general term for European
Sandhya	Worship
Sangam	Confluence of two rivers
Sannyasi	One who has abandoned all worldly possessions and affections; Brahman of the fourth order

Saphal	Successful; auspicious; fruitful; fulfilled
Sati (Suttee)	Ceremony of widow burning herself on husband's funeral pyre; a woman who does this
Satsang	Association with good and pious persons
Seer	Two pounds weight
Shilajit	Bitumen, highly esteemed as a medicine
Shraddh	Annual remembrance rite for deceased relative
Siddhi	State of perfection
Sinhasan	Throne
Swadeshi	Pertaining to one's own country; home-produced
Swami	Holy man; lord
Swaraj	Home Rule; Self Government
Tahsil	A land division for revenue and certain other purposes
Tahsildar	Officer of a tahsil
Tajbal	Thorny shrub
Tapas	Austerity
Tirtha	Holy water
Tonga	Conveyance usually drawn by one pony or a pair of bullocks
Topi	Sun-helmet
Yoga	System of philosophy; union with universal soul often by means of meditation
Yogi	Ascetic; hermit; devotee
Zamindar	Landholder; revenue farmer

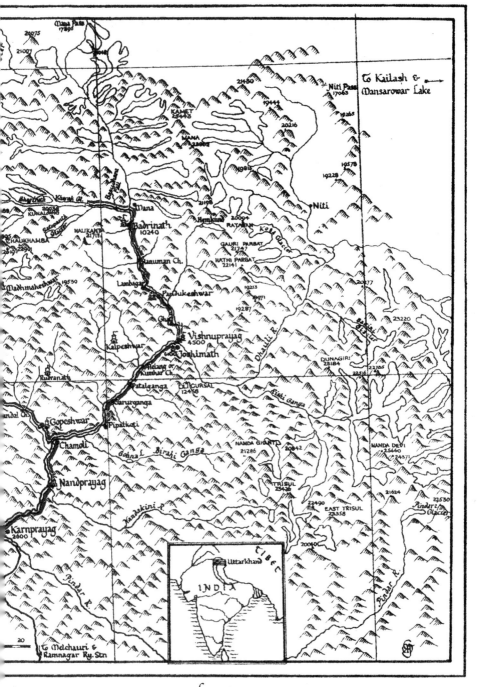

the PILGRIM ROAD
from HARDWAR (lower left)
to KEDARNATH & BADRINATH
in the north

HARDWAR
O
BADRINATH
183

HARDWAR
O
KEDARNATH
143

HARDWAR
O
GANGOTRI
154

HARDWAR
O
JAMNOTRI
153

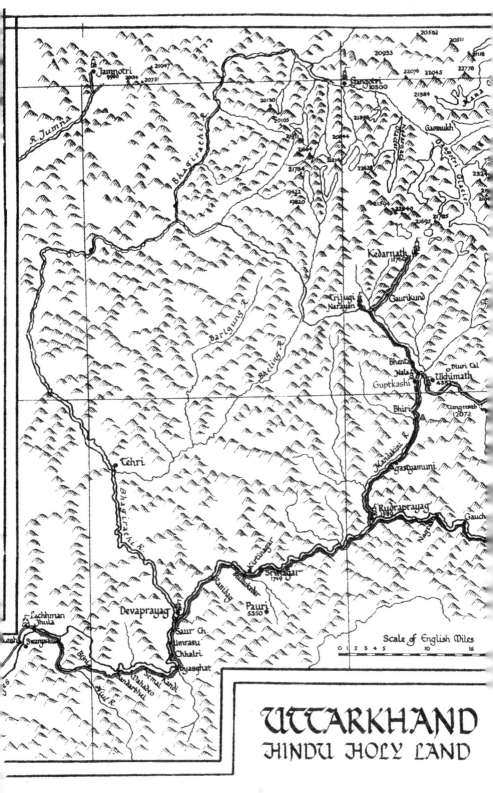

UTTARKHAND
HINDU HOLY LAND